Unders

Return this item by the last date shown.
Items may be renewed by telephone or at
www.eastrenfrewshire.gov.uk/libraries

East Renfrewshire
COUNCIL

Barrhead:	0141 577 3518	Mearns:	0141 577 4979
Busby:	0141 577 4971	Neilston:	0141 577 4981
Clarkston:	0141 577 4972	Netherlee:	0141 637 5102
Eaglesham:	0141 577 3932	Thornliebank:	0141 577 4983
Giffnock:	0141 577 4976	Uplawmoor:	01505 850564

Understand Greek Mythology

Steve Eddy and Claire Hamilton

Hodder Education

338 Euston Road, London NW1 3BH

Hodder Education is an Hachette UK company

First published in UK 2001 by Hodder Education

First published in US 2001 by The McGraw-Hill Companies, Inc.

This edition published 2012

British Library Cataloguing in Publication Data: a catalogue record
for this title is available from the British Library.

Library of Congress Catalog Card Number: on file.

10 9 8 7 6 5 4 3 2 1

Hachette UK's policy is to use papers that are natural, renewable
and recyclable products and made from wood grown in sustainable
forests. The logging and manufacturing processes are expected to
conform to the environmental regulations of the country of origin.

www.hoddereducation.co.uk

Cover image © Maksim Toome – Fotolia

Typeset by Cenveo Publisher Services

Printed in Great Britain by CPI Group (UK) Ltd, Croydon, CR0 4YY

**Also available
in ebook**

Contents

Meet the authors

Welcome to *Understand Greek Mythology*!

Our first introduction to Greek myths was in the context of their importance in the English literary heritage. Of course, we also realized that these were wonderful stories in their own right. Moreover, since they are so much a part of Western culture, to Westerners like ourselves they are both easy and satisfying to read.

However, we both became aware over the years that there was a hidden dimension to the Greek myths – and indeed all myths. This is partly thanks to our reading of authors such as Joseph Campbell, who did so much to explore the psychological depths of myths, and to point out the common threads to be found not just throughout Greek myths, but throughout myths worldwide. Carl Jung, too, has been a major influence on our thinking in his development of the concept of the collective unconscious and its archetypes. According to this thinking, the gods can be seen as elements of the psyche, while the stories told about them reflect the efforts of the collective unconscious to integrate otherwise irreconcilable drives and desires that are common to all humanity.

We have become fascinated by the recurring themes found in the Greek myths, such as the hero's quest, or the descent into the Underworld, featured, for example, in 'Orpheus and Eurydice' and 'Theseus and the Minotaur' in this book. However, what is even more compelling is the way in which these themes, in different forms, run through so much modern narrative, both in literature and in cinema, showing that they really do spring from the collective psyche.

In this book we have endeavoured to retell the myths in a lively and accessible way, while remaining faithful to the original sources. For each myth, we then offer an interpretation which we hope will demonstrate the power and significance of the myth and stimulate you to further thought and discussion.

Steve Eddy and Claire Hamilton, 2012

In one minute

Ancient Greek civilization provided the foundations of Western culture. Philosophically, artistically, scientifically and politically, the Greeks reached an astonishing level of sophistication. The deepest and most pervading expression of Greek ideology, however, lay in its mythology, which was so rich and comprehensive that its legacy has endured to the present day.

Myths are symbolic stories. They have evolved through oral tradition, and they have guided and inspired humanity for thousands of years. Down the centuries, symbols have been used to represent ideas or urges that cannot easily be defined. A symbol can magically bring an idea to life by appealing to the creative power of the imagination. It can also offer several layers of meaning in a single image.

Jung recognized the importance of mythology in psychoanalysis. In particular, he saw myths as representing the individual's journey towards psychic wholeness. Joseph Campbell, who developed this idea, wrote: 'Here we can begin to see a way of working with myths on a personal level, for our own development.' For example, when Theseus tracks down the Minotaur in the Cretan labyrinth, he lays down a thread to guide his return (see Chapter 6). Theseus' journey is the typical hero's journey – one of self-discovery. Many of the elements within it hold their own symbolic importance. This thread may symbolize divine inspiration, or the link between the conscious mind and the unconscious. The labyrinth itself can be seen as a symbol of the individual's tortuous journey to self-knowledge, and of the mysteries of the feminine.

Campbell and other writers have also pointed out that myths are still emerging and developing in the present day.

On the social level we see this in the recurrence of mythical archetypes in popular culture, for example in the hugely successful *Star Wars* films.

The aim of this book is not only to show the power of the Greek myths to entertain and enrich on a narrative level, but also to facilitate this journey to self-knowledge. It retells the myths and explores the interpretations – cultural, moral psychological and spiritual – to which they lend themselves. It also shows how the themes of Greek myths echo those of other cultures worldwide, in a way that argues for a fundamental psychic content common to all humanity.

Introduction

Mythology has been used by poets, playwrights and artists for centuries. Down the ages these timeless wisdom tales have been regarded as important expressions of humanity. However, in the nineteenth century, with the rise of scientific rationalism and of social realism in the arts, myths were in danger of being demoted to the status of quaint old stories about non-existent gods. A 'myth' began to mean simply a widely held but mistaken belief.

Myths interpreted

With the rise of psychology, however, myths found a new status – although there was controversy about their origins and functions. Sigmund Freud (1856–1939) saw them as expressing repressed impulses commonly found in the personal unconscious. For example the myth of Oedipus (see Chapter 4) expressed a boy's socially unacceptable desire to kill his father and sleep with his mother.

Claude Lévi-Strauss (1906–2009) saw myths as stemming from a human need to make sense of the world. By this model, the myths worldwide in which human beings are fashioned from clay by a divine potter, such as the Egyptian Ptah, fulfil our need to know how and why we came to be here. Other widespread myths explain death and the seasons.

Another view focuses on myth as magic. Stories of hero gods descending into the Underworld in the west, and emerging in the east, reflect the setting and rising of the sun. Myths in which an ageing goddess is reborn as a youthful virgin reflect the return of spring after winter. This kind of myth must have reassured early humanity. More important, it is likely that the repeated telling, and ritual enacting, of stories symbolizing the rising of the sun, the return of spring, or the ripening of crops was a magical way of making these things happen.

Many commentators have noted the similarities between myths in different cultures. One theory is that this can be explained by migration, trade contact, and the exchange of myths between conquerors and conquered. There is certainly some truth in this, as seen, for example, in the interweaving of Aztec and Mayan myths. However, this can hardly explain similarities such as the appearance of 'Trickster' gods in cultures across the globe: the infant Hermes stealing Apollo's cattle, the Norse Loki cutting off the golden tresses of Thor's wife, Sif, or a similarly mischievous deity of the North American Winnebago Indians.

Jung and the theory of archetypes

The exploration of myths found a new dimension in the work of Carl Jung (1875–1961). Whereas Freud saw the unconscious as being entirely personal, the product of a lifetime's repressed sexual urges, Jung identified a layer of consciousness below this – the collective unconscious. Jung regarded dreams as doorways between an individual and the collective unconscious. Many dreams, he said, expressed archetypes that might otherwise be projected onto the waking world as irrational fears, delusions or hatreds.

Jung's collective unconscious is a vast psychic pool of energized symbols shared by humanity as a whole. It is filled with 'archetypes': symbolic figures, such as the Trickster mentioned above, the Mother and the Father. They also include the animus and anima, which are the undeveloped and largely unacknowledged opposite-sex parts of, respectively, the female and male psyche. Another important archetype is the Shadow, which embodies all that we deny in ourselves and 'project' onto people we dislike. These archetypes form the dramatis personae of myth. Thus myths offer a way for cultures to explore their collective impulses, and to express them creatively, rather than harmfully.

The earliest Greek myths

Some Greek myths date back to a pre-Greek civilization, that of the Minoans, whose bull cult flourished on the island of Crete before 1600 BCE. This society was matriarchal and worshipped above all the Great Goddess or Earth Mother, who represented the fertility of the earth, the cycle of the seasons and the mysteries of life and death. She had a god consort who was linked with the starry heavens. The cult featured an anthropomorphic god figure, half-man and half-bull, who became the Greek Minotaur. Other myths deriving from ancient Crete include the birth of Zeus and the story of Europa and the bull. The Great Goddess was Hellenized into the goddess Gaia and her daughter Rhea.

Hesiod's *Theogony*

Although there was a strong oral tradition in Greece, as in most other cultures, the particular richness and complexity of Greek mythology owes much to the fact that the stories were fashioned into literature from early times. One of the first authors was Hesiod, who wrote his *Theogony* in the eighth century BCE. This was a long poem in which he attempted to collect together all the myths that had been handed down orally and organize them into a comprehensive genealogy.

Hesiod systematized various accounts of the beginning of the world into three distinct generations of deities. Starting with Gaia, the Great Goddess of the earth who emanated from Chaos, he told how the world began. This myth of Creation is recounted in detail in the first story in this book, which also tells how Uranus devoured his and Gaia's offspring, before being outwitted by his son, Cronus. After this, Cronus was outwitted, in turn, by his son Zeus, who divided the universe into three parts, giving Poseidon the sea and Hades the Underworld, while he himself took over the earth and became ruler of the 12 gods and goddesses who dwelt on Mount Olympus.

The five races

In another poem, *Works and Days*, Hesiod speaks of five races of man. The first was the Golden race, who lived at the time of Cronus. They were like gods, living free from misery, pain and strife. Ageless but not immortal, they died easily in their sleep, after which they became pure spirits, inhabiting the upper levels, and able to protect men. After them came a feebler Silver race who were childish and failed to honour the gods. These, too, passed away, but became the blessed spirits of the Underworld. Next came the Bronze race, made from ash trees. They were fearsome and strong, wearing bronze armour, living in bronze houses and using bronze implements. They were so bellicose, however, that they ended up killing each other, whereupon they descended wholesale into Hades. After this came the Hero race. These were

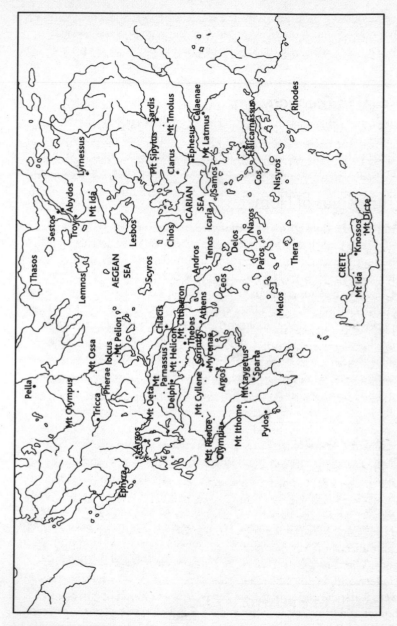

Figure 0.1 Map of ancient Greece

demigods and included all the great Greek heroes. Some died normally, but others, like Heracles, were taken to the Islands of the Blessed, which were ruled by Cronus. The last race of men was the present 'Iron' one. This was the most piteous race, but at least it could call on the heroes and the beneficent spirits of the upper and lower regions.

Hesiod, however, was not a creative artist like Homer, but an organizer. His work in collecting and systematizing the myths is invaluable, but some of the accounts contradict each other and in some places, too, he indulges in some personal-sounding homilies.

The genius of Homer

In Hesiod's fourth race of men are found the incomparable heroes of Greek tradition, whose attributes of prowess, fearlessness and honour were a dominant theme in the myths and inspired the literature of Homer. His two great epic poems, the *Iliad* and the *Odyssey*, are thought to have been composed towards the end of the eighth century BCE. The *Iliad* chiefly recounts events that took place during the Trojan War, concentrating on key heroic figures such as Achilles, Agamemnon and Hector, while the *Odyssey* relates the adventures of Odysseus on his return journey from Troy.

Although he used historical material, Homer's purpose was not so much to record past events as to give an exciting account of heroic action. In this respect, Homer has been called the father of the modern novel. In its blend of history and mythology, the *Odyssey*, in particular, shows his genius as a storyteller. Its purpose was clearly not so much to instruct mankind as to capture the imagination and glorify Odysseus. The gods have an ambiguous role in it, being seen as capricious and inconstant, both in their dealings with each other and with mortals. Indeed, part of Odysseus' prowess involves his attempts at outwitting them. The complex relationship between the gods and heroes was a feature of Homer's epics and has continued to be a source of fascination in subsequent retellings of the myths.

The role of the hero

More often than not, the subject of Greek myths is heroic. The role of the hero is mapped out in such recurring themes as the separation from the mother, the overcoming of obstacles, and the finding and supplanting of the father. The great heroes whose lives conform to this pattern include Perseus, Theseus, Jason and Oedipus.

Of these, Perseus (see Chapter 5) can be seen as the most faultless of the Greek heroes. He achieves his quest early on in his career through a combination of the aid of the gods and his own prowess. Then, after winning his bride Andromeda, he nobly gives away his kingdom and rules elsewhere. After this he kills his grandfather by accident and through a trial of skill. In this he fulfils a prophecy revealed by an oracle, but incurs no penalty.

In the degree to which the other heroes depart from this ideal, their lives suffer. For example, after Theseus abandons Ariadne he becomes embroiled in a string of bad relationships, including a disastrous attempt to abduct Persephone. Jason, too, suffers in his relationships with women because of a failure of discrimination, while Oedipus is flawed by his temper and his attempts to escape his fate. The story of Oedipus, however, is a telling example of the way in which the Greeks believed character and fate were inextricably linked. All Oedipus' efforts to avoid his fate serve only to bind him deeper within it.

Interestingly, Odysseus, who is perhaps the most famous Greek hero of all, does not conform in any way to the heroic pattern. His fame rests as much on his cunning as on his strength. Although Homer portrayed Odysseus as heroic and honourable, later writers, such as Euripides and Virgil, chose to emphasize his wiliness. Like Jason, however, Odysseus finds that his voyages are protracted through the hindrance of a god whom he has angered – in his case Poseidon.

Destiny

In Greek myths, human beings are subject to the gods, and to fate, which is why it was thought to be possible to discover one's destiny from oracles like the one at Delphi. Hence, some characters in the myths try to avoid their fate but fail to do so. Oedipus, for example, tries to avoid killing his father and sleeping with his mother, but still does so because he is unaware that he was adopted. Perseus' grandfather Acrisius tries to outwit the prediction that he will be killed by his own grandson, but in the end fate proves to be inescapable. Despite their great powers, all the gods, even Zeus, were subject to a higher authority, that of Moros, or Destiny, which had been created by Night. In their seemingly capricious acts of helping or hindering a hero, the gods often found themselves unwittingly conforming to his fate.

A hero's destiny was commonly revealed by oracles, prophecies or dreams, but was often so obscure that it could be only partly understood. Any attempts he made to outwit it were doomed to failure and might even serve to hasten the dreaded event. Tragedy often arose from a misunderstanding or failure to bow to fate.

Greek tragedy

The myths were also the subjects of the famous Greek dramas that were performed at the great festival held annually at Athens during the fifth century BCE. The three great tragedians – Aeschylus, Sophocles and Euripides –wrote hundreds of plays between them, of which only a fraction survive. Their dramas show the hero trapped between the conflicting powers of fate and the gods, and also subject to his own strengths and weaknesses. A favourite tragic theme is the fall of the great man. The main characters in the plays are seen as symbolic of mankind rather than as individuals. To this end, masks were used and the great poetic utterances of the characters were challenged or reflected by the Greek chorus. The themes were weighty and the plays were long. In fact, very often a theme, such as that of revenge, would be carried through a trilogy of plays as, for example, in Aeschylus' *The Oresteia*. Sophocles' great surviving trilogy concerns the fate of Oedipus, while Euripides took a more psychological approach, examining the agonies and passions of such tormented women as Electra and Medea.

The afterlife

The ancient Greeks seem to have held several conflicting beliefs concerning the afterlife. Although there is no disputing the continued existence of souls, there are a variety of destinations given for them, Hades being the most usual. This was a gloomy place where the souls of the dead appeared only as shades. It was ruled by the god Hades with his wife, Persephone. But Hades was not a devil and there was no sense of evil attached to his realm. It was bounded by the river

Styx, and all dead souls who had received proper burial were carried across it by Charon, the ferryman, on payment of the appropriate fee. At the gates lay Cerberus, a hound who devoured anyone trying to escape. Although the Underworld was not generally given over to torments and punishments, it was nevertheless shadowy and depressing. A few brave heroes dared to go down to Hades while living and returned again. The most famous included Orpheus, Heracles, Odysseus and Theseus. When Odysseus visited Hades, he met Achilles, who told him he would rather be living, in however humble a capacity, than remain there.

In Hades there was also a place for offenders called Tartarus. Here, famously were found Sisyphus, Ixion and Tantalus undergoing different forms of punishment. Later writers also located Elysium in Hades. This was a blessed place where a few favoured mortals were sent. It compares with the Isles of the Blessed, where Heracles is supposed to have gone and seems to have much in common with the Celtic Otherworld.

The Greeks also believed in a form of reincarnation. For example, the fifth-century-BCE poet Pindar, writing of the Isles of the Blessed, says that as well as heroes residing there, it was also the abode of those who had lived justly for three incarnations. The Eleusinian and other Mystery religions (see below) offered followers the hope of ending up in a better place than Hades and perhaps of attaining Elysium.

The myth of Er

There is also a more elaborate concept of the afterlife, reported by the philosopher Plato in his *Republic*. This is the myth of Er, a complex story that may have come from the Orphic Mysteries. In it a Pamphylian soldier, named Er, dies in battle but is later revived and tells how his psyche or soul journeyed in company with others, and came to a place of four chasms, two in the sky and two in the earth. After judgement, some ascended to the heavens and were later brought back cleansed, others descended into the Underworld and were punished tenfold for their evils, while those who could not be redeemed were flung into the deepest depths of Tartarus. Er then described a tall rainbow-coloured column connecting earth and heaven, which was attached to a spindle resting in the lap of Necessity. Eight ascending spheres revolved around the column and on each was a Siren who sang a continuous note, all eight forming a musical scale. Around the pillar sat the three Fates, daughters of Necessity: Lachesis, Clotho and Atropos representing respectively past, present and future.

The souls had to go before Lachesis, who, as the Disposer of Lots, made them each choose their next life, which could be human or animal. Among the souls who had to choose were the heroes: Ajax, who chose to be a lion; Orpheus, who chose a swan; Agamemnon, who chose an eagle, and Odysseus, who chose the quiet life of a common man. After this the souls were allotted Guardian Angels who led them to Clotho with her whirling spindle, who ratified each lot, and then to Atropos, who spun the threads of destiny, and made each choice irreversible. After this the souls passed to the plain of Lethe where they were made to drink from the Waters of Forgetfulness. All this was shown to Er and explained by an Interpreter. He was then despatched back into his body and found himself on his funeral pyre.

The Mystery religions

Plato, in relating the story of Er, commented that, if a man lived wisely, he could hope that his journey after death would not take him over 'the stony ground of the Underworld but along the smooth road of heaven'. How to attain this was the subject of the Mysteries. The Mysteries were intimately bound up with the myths because they were enacted in their rituals. In fact, it is not known whether the myths came from the rituals or the rituals from the myths. However, as the partakers of the Mysteries were forbidden to speak of their experiences on pain of death, very little is known of them. Nevertheless, some information has been gleaned from Christian writers and there are also well-preserved paintings on the wall of the House of the Mysteries in Pompeii (see Chapter 1). Although the Mystery religions became increasingly popular after 300 BCE when belief in the old gods was beginning to wane, some, like those at Eleusis (modern Eleusina), were very ancient, probably dating back to before 1000 BCE.

The Eleusinian Mysteries were the most famous of all the Mysteries and were attended by thousands of initiates and would-be initiates who travelled from the whole of Greece and beyond to take part in them.

In fact, a truce was regularly called for 55 days to allow safe travel to and from them. Unusually, initiation was open to all: men and women, Athenians and foreigners, slaves and freemen alike. The Mysteries were connected to Demeter and were concerned with the death and regeneration of the crops and, on a symbolic level, with all of humanity. (For a fuller description of the Eleusinian Mysteries, see Chapter 8.)

Literary sources

As we have seen, from early times the Greeks gave their myths literary form. They then evolved artistically for a thousand years or so and in the process were refined and elaborated more than has been the case with other cultures. In consequence, early literary works concerning them are numerous and provide a rich mine of story and information. A chronological list of some of the ancient authors is given below:

Key ancient sources for the Greek myths

Homer   Epic poet, c. 750–700 BCE
Works: *Iliad*, *Odyssey*

Hesiod   Poet, c. 700 BCE
Works include: *Theogony*, *Works and Days*

Aeschylus   Tragic playwright c. 525–456 BCE
Works include: *Seven against Thebes*, *Oresteia*, *Prometheus Bound*

Pindar   Lyric poet c. 518–438 BCE
Works include: Choral odes sung at the Olympian, Pythian, Nemean and Isthmian games

Sophocles   Tragic playwright c. 496–406 BCE
Works include: *Oedipus Rex*, *Oedipus at Colonus*, *Antigone*

Euripides   Tragic playwright c. 480–406 BCE
Works include: *Medea*, *Electra*, *The Trojan Women*, *The Bacchae*

Plato   Philosopher c. 427–347 BCE
Works include: *The Republic*, *The Symposium*

Apollonius of Rhodes   Epic poet, third century BCE
Works: *Argonautica*

Apollodorus   Scholar *c*. 180–120 BCE
Works: *Library* – erroneously attributed to him, being written first or second century CE

Virgil   Roman poet 70–19 BCE
Works include: *The Aeneid*, *Georgics*

Plutarch   Philosopher, biographer *c*. 50 BCE – 120 CE
Works: *Moralia*, *Parallel Lives*

Ovid   Roman poet 43 BCE–17 CE
Works include: *Metamorphoses*, *Art of Love*

Pausanias   Writer of second century CE
Works: *Description of Greece*

Many of these texts can be found on the Perseus Project website (see Select Bibliography).

1

The gods and goddesses

Greek mythology, like the mythology of some other cultures, features both an older pantheon of gods and a newer one which supplanted it, possibly reflecting a shift from an earth-based matriarchal religion to a sky-based patriarchal one. The original pantheon includes the earth goddess Gaia (whose name has been adopted by the modern ecology movement) and her child and consort, Uranus, and their children. Two of these children, Cronus and Rhea, became the parents of a new generation of gods. The foremost of these, Zeus, led the new generation of gods in battle against the old, rather as the Babylonian sky god Marduk led one set of gods against another to establish his ascendancy. Zeus and most of the gods of his generation were said to reside on Mount Olympus, which is the highest mountain in Greece. It is these Olympian gods who feature most strongly in surviving Greek myths.

Insight

The gods were differentiated from the heroes not so much by their strength as by their supernatural power. They demanded worship from heroes and men alike and, in return, were able to perform miracles, offer supernatural protection, or give magical gifts – as in the story of Perseus (see Chapter 5).

Each of the 12 Olympians possesses a distinctive character:

Zeus	God of thunder and ruler of the gods
Poseidon	God of the sea
Hephaestus	Smith god
Hermes	Messenger of the gods
Ares	God of war
Apollo	God of light, sometimes connected with Helios, the sun.
Dionysus	God of wine and fertility

Hera	Wife of Zeus and queen of the gods
Athene	Goddess of wisdom and war
Artemis	The virgin huntress
Demeter	Earth Mother and goddess of grain
Aphrodite	Goddess of love

In addition to these Olympian deities were Hades, who ruled the Underworld with his queen, Persephone, and also the dark goddess Hecate, who lived with them. Hestia, goddess of the hearth, originally one of the Olympians, was replaced by Dionysus in the fifth century BCE.

Zeus was god of the sky, thunder and lightning. He reigned supreme and had the power to punish the other gods if they displeased him. He had a famous sanctuary at Dodona, in Epirus, where a sacred oak gave out oracles and was attended by a priesthood. He also had a great temple on Olympus (a town in the Peloponnese) which contained a seated statue of him, nearly 40 feet high, carved by the sculptor Phidias. Although married to **Hera**, the goddess of marriage and childbirth, Zeus had numerous affairs with nymphs and mortal women, sometimes taking the guise of animals such as a bull, or even a shower of gold, in order to get his way. Hera was extremely jealous and spent much of her time punishing the unfortunate recipients of his love. Many of them, however, gave birth to demigods or heroes.

Both **Poseidon** and **Hermes** are thought to be very ancient gods, probably older than Zeus. Poseidon was extremely powerful, being able to cause storms and even earthquakes. Besides being the sea god, he was also connected with horses. Among his numerous offspring was the hero Theseus, and Polyphemus the Cyclops. Hermes was equally powerful but more subtly so. He was the messenger of Zeus, being a master of travel and communication. He was also able to transcend the boundaries of the upper and lower worlds, for he was a 'psychopomp' – a conveyer of souls to the realm of Hades. He had something of the Trickster figure about him, too, being mischievous and cunning. Although he never took a wife, he had numerous affairs and fathered many children, including the pastoral god Pan. Statues of Hermes with an erect phallus, and known as 'herms', were often set up at crossroads as they were believed to bring good fortune.

Although **Ares** and **Athene** both represented war, they differed from each other. Ares was hot-blooded and violent, and Zeus liked him least of all. But he was handsome enough to attract Aphrodite, with whom he had an affair and who afterwards gave birth to Eros. Ares was associated with the Golden Fleece, which was hung in a grove sacred to him. By contrast, Athene was cool-headed and wise, using war mostly as a means of defence. She was the daughter of Zeus, having been born, fully armed, from his head. Her mother was Metis, 'thought', and this is where her wisdom came from. She was a virgin goddess and also a goddess of the arts and even of peacemaking. Being wise, she was associated with the owl. The Parthenon in Athens was her temple.

Apollo was at first the god of light, later becoming merged with Helios, the sun god. He was also god of inspiration, music, healing and prophecy. He was adept at playing the lyre. He had a shrine at Delphi which he set up after killing the Python, a fearsome serpent or dragon which had formerly inhabited the shrine. This action was interpreted as the victory of light over the Underworld force of darkness, for which he was afterwards called Pythian Apollo. From his shrine came many famous oracles, including the well-known prophecy about Oedipus and also the instruction to Orestes to kill his mother, Clytemnestra. Apollo shared his shrine with Dionysus, who lived there in the winter while Apollo was away in the far north. Depicted as eternally beautiful and youthful, Apollo had many loves, especially among the nymphs. Nevertheless, some resisted him, the most famous being Daphne, who turned into a laurel tree. Apollo was also accompanied by the nine Muses of poetic inspiration.

Insight

Thirty-three *Hymns* to the gods survive which were erroneously attributed to Homer (and hence are often known as the 'Homeric Hymns'). These were sung at festivals in praise of their deeds, their beauty and their power.

Demeter and her daughter **Persephone**, were ancient matriarchal deities, connected with the land and the turning seasons. The main story concerning them is the abduction of Persephone by Hades. Demeter also set up the famous Eleusinian Mysteries (see below). **Artemis**, the virgin huntress, was connected with Demeter, being, paradoxically, patron of childbirth. She could be harsh and vengeful, quick to punish those who failed to honour her. She was also connected with Hecate, both being associated with the moon. Her great temple at Ephesus was one of the seven wonders of the world.

Aphrodite, the goddess of love, was the most provocative of the gods. From the beginning she was accompanied by Eros, the abstract force of desire, who later became personified as her son. She was married to Hephaestus, the lame smith god who was also the god of fire, but she preferred the well-formed Ares, with whom she had an affair. She also slept with Hermes but her great love was the beautiful boy, Adonis. She famously won the prize for beauty when Paris was made to judge between her, Hera and Athene. But the ensuing jealousy of the other two goddesses led to the Trojan War. Aphrodite herself frequently and capriciously used the power of love to stir up strife, for instance, when she made Hades fall in love with Persephone. Her powers were therefore seen as ultimately disruptive and often leading to war. In this respect, it is interesting to note that Ares was the father of Eros. Aphrodite was connected with Cyprus, having been born off the coast near Paphos.

Dionysus, the god of wine, was the son of Zeus by the mortal Semele. Born untimely, he was carried to term in his father's thigh and so became known as the 'twice-born'. He was at first pursued by the jealous Hera, who drove him mad so that he wandered the earth, going as far as Egypt and Syria. Cured of his madness, he was nevertheless associated with disorder. He had his own cult and was worshipped in festivals which promoted drunkenness and licentiousness. His followers were the female Maenads, who became so frenzied that they would tear animals to pieces, as well as any men who happened to come their way when the fit was on them.

The Dionysian festivals featured enactments of the stories of the god which became the origin of Greek drama. Dionysus is supposed to have married Ariadne, after Theseus deserted her on Naxos. Curiously, Dionysus also had a second identity. The drunken, mature man evolved, paradoxically, into the young boy of light, who was connected with regeneration. In this respect, a conflicting account of his origins says that Zeus took the form of a snake and impregnated Persephone. As the son of Persephone, therefore, he became part of the famous Eleusinian Mysteries. He was also connected with the Orphic Mysteries (see Chapter 9).

The Dionysiac Mysteries

The wall paintings in the House of the Mysteries in Pompeii are remarkably well-preserved and show various initiations carried out against a bright-red background. These are thought to be representations of the Dionysiac Mysteries and show scenes of ritual offerings, music-playing, a woman feeding a kid goat from her breast, a satyr with a grotesque mask, a woman unveiling a large phallus, a woman being whipped, the same woman dancing with cymbals and, finally, a scene representing the mystical marriage. Like those at Eleusis, these Mysteries are also thought to be dealing with the theme of death and resurrection, requiring the initiate to undergo various tests and trials in order to achieve mystical understanding. The Dionysiac Mysteries were said to have been set up by Orpheus, but he also had his own Mysteries which were linked to those of Dionysus.

KEEP IN MIND...

1 Greek mythology features an older pantheon of gods and a newer one which supplanted it. The older pantheon includes Gaia and Uranus, and their children. Two of these, Cronus and Rhea, became the parents of the new generation of gods.

2 Zeus led the new generation of Olympian gods to triumph against the old gods. This may represent a shift from a matriarchal religion to a patriarchal one.

3 Zeus' brothers were Poseidon, who ruled the sea, and Hades, who ruled the Underworld.

4 Hera was Zeus' wife; Persephone was the wife of Hades.

5 Hephaestus, the lame smith god, was married to Aphrodite, goddess of love, who had an affair with Ares, the god of war.

6 Hermes was the messenger of the gods, known for his intelligence and trickery.

7 Apollo was the god of light, connected with Helios, the sun. He was also the god of prophecy and a patron of the arts.

8 Dionysus was god of wine and fertility. He was associated with the Dionysiac Mysteries.

9 Athene and Artemis were virgin goddesses. Athene was the goddess of wisdom and the art of war; Artemis the goddess of hunting.

10 Demeter was Earth Mother, goddess of grain, and the mother of Persephone.

The beginning of time

This version of the main Greek creation myth is largely taken from Hesiod's *Theogony* and *Works and Days*, with some details introduced from the later writers Apollodorus, Apollonius and Pausanias. There is general agreement on the basic story, with some differences in the locations of events. More significantly, Apollodorus plays down the importance of Gaia, making Uranus simply the 'first ruler of the world', who takes Gaia to wife, rather than being her son. Likewise, Apollodorus states that the Furies spring directly from Uranus' blood, rather than from Gaia's womb.

There are also versions of the myth, for example mentioned by Pausanias, in which the reign of Cronus is a Golden Age among men. These are likely to have evolved from versions in which the vanquished Cronus is 'pensioned off' to rule a Land of the Blessed (something like the Celtic Tir na nóg, the dwelling place of dead heroes), located somewhere near the setting sun.

First to enter into existence was Chaos, simply a vast, dark and yawning emptiness. Into this emptiness soon came Gaia, the great Earth, sure foundation of the great gods who live on snow-capped Olympus. Into this universe there came, too, the murky depths of Tartarus, and the bright love god Eros, who unsettles even the minds of the wise.

From Chaos, too, there came forth the Underworld region of Erebus and black Night. They coupled, and Night gave birth to Aether and Day. Then Gaia brought forth Uranus, the starry god of the heavens, her equal, to embrace her on every side. And she brought forth long hills, to be frequented by graceful nymphs, and the fruitless depths of the raging salt-sea, Pontus.

So far Gaia had produced these beings without the sweet union of love. Now, however, she lay with Uranus, and from this union of Earth and Sky sprang deep-swirling Oceanus, god of the river that encircles the Earth. Other children followed: the brothers Coeus, Crius and Iapetus, and Hyperion – who was to become father of the Sun and Moon; and sisters, Theia and Rhea, Themis and Mnemosyne, golden-crowned Phoebe and beautiful Tethys. Last-born of the Titans, but definitely not least, was the wily Cronus, who detested his father Uranus.

Now Gaia bore the terrible one-eyed Cyclopes – Brontes, Steropes and stubborn Arges, and then the Hundred-Handers – the fearsome giants Cottus, Briareos and Gyes, who each had a hundred unapproachable arms and fifty heads.

Uranus hated all his offspring, and so as each was born into the light, he thrust them back into the dark and secret womb of Gaia. She grieved for her children and groaned with the fullness of her womb. When this became too much to bear, she spoke to her children: 'My children, we should punish the vile crimes of your father, for he is the first who ever thought of doing shameful things.'

All were afraid, and would not answer their mother. But then Cronus, the youngest and most cunning of the Titans, took heart and replied: 'Mother, I will undertake this deed, for I do not respect our father. He is the first who ever thought of doing shameful things.'

So Earth rejoiced, and placed in her son's hands a saw-toothed sickle which she had made from the hardest flint. Then she hid him where he lay waiting to ambush Uranus, and told him what to do.

That night, Uranus the starry sky lay down upon Gaia in longing for love, little suspecting the fate that awaited him. As he lay in deep union with Gaia, Cronus, full of loathing for his father, stretched out his left hand from his hiding place in the womb of Gaia. He wielded the sharp-toothed sickle and hacked off his father's genitals, hurling them away behind him, separating Sky from Earth once and for all.

The blood of Uranus gushed onto the Earth, impregnating her, and in due course of time she gave birth to the powerful Erinyes – the Furies – to armed giants, and to the nymphs called the Meliae. The discarded genitals fell into the restless sea, and after a while they gathered around them a white foam – *aphros* – out of which grew the lovely Aphrodite.

The mighty Cronus now reigned supreme, but proved to be no kinder than his father Uranus. He forcibly took to wife his sister Rhea, and she bore him great children: goddesses Hestia, Demeter and golden-slippered Hera, pitiless Hades, stern Poseidon and wise Zeus the Thunderer, father of gods. Cronus, though mighty, feared Gaia's prophecy that he would be overthrown by one of his children. But he did not thrust them back into the earth like his father. Instead, as each child was born he swallowed it whole.

Rhea grieved constantly for her devoured children. Then, one day, when she was about to give birth to almighty Zeus, she asked her parents for help. Acting on their advice, she travelled by night to the land of Crete. There she gave birth to her son and gave him to her mother, Gaia, to care for and protect. Gaia hid the boy-god in a huge cave hidden beneath a thickly forested mountain. To Cronus, whose turn it now was to be tricked, Rhea gave a huge boulder wrapped in swaddling clothes. Unsuspecting, he took it and swallowed it as he had done the other children, thinking his position still secure.

While the tyrant continued to rule, the young Zeus grew up in the cave, attended by the nymphs Adrasteia and Ida. At first, the Curetes protected him by dancing outside the cave and making such a noise by clashing their spears and shields that Cronus could not hear the infant's cries. But the time came when Zeus grew to manhood, and with Gaia's help he forced Cronus to vomit up the children filling his belly – preceded by the huge stone substituted for Zeus himself, which the Thunderer placed at Pythos as a monument.

Zeus freed the grateful Cyclopes and the Hundred-Handers from murky Tartarus, where they had been imprisoned by scheming Cronus. Together they fought long and hard against Cronus and those Titans who remained loyal to him, an old guard challenged by young gods. The fighting was fierce. The seas boiled, the mountains shook and flames leapt up all around as the two generations of gods did battle. Finally the strength of the Hundred-Handers tipped the balance, and mighty Zeus was able to imprison the Titans in Tartarus.

Zeus, however, had one more adversary to contend with – and a powerful one at that. Angry at the imprisonment of the Titans, Gaia mated with Tartarus and produced a terrible monster, Typhon, to challenge her grandson. This creature was taller than all mountains, and had snakes' heads for fingers. He was winged and fire-breathing, and his body from the thighs down was composed of writhing serpents. The hundred snake-heads on his shoulders were able to produce any terrible sound, from the bellowing of bulls to the roaring of lions. The monster and Zeus met in a final terrible conflagration, but Zeus was able to scorch all the monster's heads with his thunderbolts. When Typhon collapsed, crippled, Zeus hurled him into Tartarus. His reign was now secure.

Commentary

Most cultures have myths which attempt to explain how the universe began. One of the ways in which they differ is in their starting point, or what they take as being fundamental. The biblical Genesis starts with a god who creates the sky and earth; the Hopi Indian creation starts with Taiowa, who resides in Endless Space; the Chinese myth of Pangu starts with darkness, the rule of Chaos, and a cosmic egg, out of which the giant Pangu hatches. The Greek myth is in a sense very sophisticated in that it goes back to first principles: 'a vast, dark and yawning emptiness'. This is not chaos in the modern sense of disorder, because there is as yet nothing to be ordered: there is no form, just potential. Indeed, in some variants of the myth there is a cosmic egg, a symbol of contained potential, out of which everything hatches – rather in the manner of the Big Bang that astrophysicists describe as forming the universe. Another view of the Greek beginning is that it is female, or *yin*; the masculine, or *yang*, world of form emerges from it.

Insight

The image of potential contained in the 'cosmic egg' of Chaos relates to findings in astrophysics suggesting no complete vacuum can exist, and that even in an apparent vacuum there is a 'field of potential' out of which particles spontaneously appear.

In the version of the story given above, the first being to emerge from Chaos is female – Gaia. As with many primal goddess–consort pairings, Uranus is her son as well as her husband. Together they provide a metaphor with several meanings. Uranus is spirit, sky and consciousness; Gaia is matter, earth and the unconscious. At this early stage of mythic development, there is no distinction between the gods and the universe; when the starry night sky seems to envelop the earth, Uranus is coupling with Gaia. This relationship is mirrored in other cultures; usually the sky is male and the earth female, though in the Egyptian variant it is the other way round: Nut the sky goddess arches over the earth god Geb and suckles him from above.

SEPARATION AND FALL

The separation of earth and sky occurs in creation myths worldwide, probably representing the stage of human development when the conscious mind began to separate from the unconscious. In the Chinese myth, the lighter parts of the cosmic egg form the sky, the denser parts the earth. Pangu fears that they may reunite, and so he stands between them, forcing them apart as he grows, until in the end he falls asleep, and then dies, from the effort. The Polynesian myth of Rangi and Papa brings the Greek and Chinese myths together. Sky god Rangi is locked in a permanent embrace with earth goddess Papa. The young gods complain that there is no room for anything to live or grow on earth (or in another version the divine embrace continually grinds creatures to death). They try to separate Rangi and Papa, but only the forest god Tane is able to do so, by standing, like Pangu, rooted in the earth and growing, slowly forcing them apart.

The Greek version is more dramatic. When Cronus severs his father's genitals, parting sky and earth, this signifies a sudden leap of human development from unconscious to self-conscious. On the level of the individual, this change occurs in childhood, either gradually, as in the Polynesian and Chinese myths, or suddenly, as in the Greek. It is also interesting that it is Cronus who wields the sickle. He is the Greek god of time (from whom the word 'chronology' is derived), and his symbolic act separates humanity from nature by making it self-conscious. Humanity emerges from the realm of the eternal into the world of time, now aware of past and future, no longer living in the eternal moment. This is, in fact, comparable to the biblical Fall.

Insight

The violent separation of earth and sky in the Greek myth of Uranus and Gaia, and in other myths worldwide, suggests that the development of human consciousness – and self-consciousness, including the awareness of time and the inevitability of one's death – necessitated a 'loss of innocence', a separation from nature. Human self-awareness makes art and philosophy possible, but it also distances us from the rest of the universe.

SACRIFICE

In many creation myths there is an element of self-sacrifice. The body of the Chinese giant Pangu becomes the physical world, as does the body of the Norse giant Ymir, and the Babylonian monster-goddess Tiamat, slain by the young god-hero Marduk. The Lakota Sioux creator god Inyan sacrifices his own blood and regenerative power to create the world. Uranus is in a sense sacrificed for the good of the world, albeit unwillingly. His blood gives rise to the Furies, and out of his genitals, mingling with the sea, comes Aphrodite. So, out of a violent act of separation spring two types of goddess: the Furies' principle is revenge, and Aphrodite's is the harmonizing of disparate elements, particularly through sexual union – or, in the context of this myth, sexual *re*union.

Insight

In Christianity the crucifixion of Jesus Christ reflects myths of cosmic sacrifice for the good of the universe and humanity, such as that of Uranus.

SUCCESSIVE PANTHEONS

Many cultures have myths in which new gods replace old. The Babylonian myth of Marduk and Tiamat (see above) is an example. The Greek myth contains three generations of gods. This may reflect historical waves of migration and conquest, and there is also a strong element of matriarchy warring with patriarchy (see Chapter 4). We certainly see the matriarchal principle in the desire of Gaia and Rhea to save the lives of their children. They champion the renewal of life, which is linked to the drive of the new generation of gods to usurp the old, and the son's drive to supplant the father. The father, especially Cronus, can also be seen as the self-preserving ego, fighting against change. However, the succession of pantheons also points to the successive stages of human development towards consciousness, civilization and social justice.

It is also interesting that Zeus is hidden in a cave in the earth, which is like a womb: the female element is necessary for his survival. Moreover, Rhea's feeding of a stone to Cronus in place of the child can be seen as a mockery of male inability to produce children – which is also found in the fairy tale of Little Red Riding Hood, in which the Wolf has stones stitched into his belly.

Insight

Leonard Shlain, in *The Alphabet versus the Goddess*, characterizes matriarchy as inclusive and non-judgemental, and patriarchy as exclusive and judgemental.

ZEUS AS HERO

The cosmic violence that erupts at the end of the myth could hint at the collective unconscious harbouring a knowledge of the violent beginnings of the universe, with antimatter warring with matter and eventually being cast into the darkness of Tartarus. It could also relate to later, cultural conflicts. Zeus emerges not only as the head of the new order of gods, the Olympians, but as a hero on the lines of Marduk. He grows from upstart revolutionary to undisputed patriarchal authority. This is very much a model of the development of Greek civilization, from the 'feminine' world of instinct and the unconscious, to the 'male' world of conscious, rational thought. Remnants of the old order are firmly suppressed, cast into Tartarus. However, the old and once-mighty powers are not dead; they are merely imprisoned within the underworld of the unconscious.

KEEP IN MIND...

1 The universe began with Chaos, a dark emptiness. Out of Chaos came the goddess Gaia, the underworld Tartarus, the love god Eros, Erebus (Darkness) and Night. Erebus and Night mated, giving birth to Aether and Day.

2 Gaia then brought forth the sky god Uranus to be her consort, the earth and everything on it, and the sea – Pontus. She then lay with Uranus and gave birth to a whole pantheon of gods – the Titans. The last-born, Cronus, hated Uranus.

3 Gaia then bore the Cyclopes, and then the Hundred-Handers – fearsome giants.

4 Uranus hated his offspring, so he thrust each in turn back into Gaia's womb. But Cronus took a sickle provided by Gaia and hacked off his father's genitals, hurling them into the sea, separating sky from earth. From the blood of Uranus sprang the Furies, and from his genitals came Aphrodite.

5 Cronus took his sister Rhea to wife and produced the first Olympian gods: Hestia, Demeter, Hera, Hades, Poseidon and Zeus. He ate all his children except Zeus, for whom Rhea substituted a stone. When Zeus grew up, he made Cronus vomit up his children, then led them in battle against Cronus and the Titans, and finally the monster Typhon. Zeus defeated them and established the reign of the Olympians.

6 The myth of Chaos begins with potential – Nothing rather than Something. It can be connected with some of the findings of astrophysics about how the universe began.

7 The Greek creation myth is one of several worldwide featuring successive pantheons.

8 Gaia and Rhea represent the matriarchal principle in their desire to preserve life. Uranus and Cronus represent the self-preserving ego, resisting change.

9 Rhea's substitution of a stone for the infant Zeus can be seen as a mockery of male inability to give birth.

10 Zeus emerges as the all-conquering hero, head of the Olympian pantheon, and father of the gods.

Echo and Narcissus

This myth is most famously found in Ovid's *Metamorphoses*. It is also mentioned by Pausanias in his *Description of Greece*.

The 'wave-blue water nymph' Liriope was once ravished by the river god Cephisus and bore a beautiful son whom she named Narcissus. She asked Tiresias the prophet what fate was in store for the boy. Would he live long and be contented? Tiresias replied with typical prophetic ambiguity: 'Only if he shall not know himself.'

The boy grew up possessed of a beauty which had a maidenly quality to it. By his mid-teens the characteristics of manhood and boyhood were perfectly combined in him. He was lithe and sinewy yet his skin was soft; he was quick and skilful at hunting, wary when stalking his prey, yet his eyes were like pools of shining innocence. Both young men and girls fell helplessly under his spell, desiring his love. But Narcissus was proud and haughty and held himself aloof from others, disdaining love.

One day when he was hunting deer he became separated from his companions and wandered into unfamiliar woodland haunted by a nymph named Echo. Echo had once been the lively-tongued companion of the great goddess Hera, wife of Zeus. But once, in a bid to keep peace between that quarrelsome couple, she had used her gift of entertaining speech as a delaying tactic so that Hera would not discover her husband enjoying the embraces of a group of young nymphs. When Hera discovered Echo's deception, she turned her quick temper on her, cursing her tongue and decreeing that she would never again be able to initiate speech. All she would allow her was to copy the last words uttered by another voice.

Echo saw Narcissus and, like many before her, instantly fell in love with his beauty of form and face. When he called out 'Anyone here?'

she straightaway answered 'Here!' Unable to see anyone, he called again, 'Come this way!', to which she replied, 'This way!' Following her voice he ventured farther into the forest, calling 'Why run away?' to which she repeated 'Why run away?' At last he stopped, baffled and called out, 'Join me here!'

Joyfully echoing his words, the nymph ran to him and put her arms round his neck. Narcissus jumped back in horror, shouting at her to keep her arms away and swearing 'I'd rather die than yield to you!' To which the nymph echoed sadly, 'Yield to you,' before turning and running, desolate and ashamed into the heart of the woods. After that she lingered among lonely caves, feeding on her grief, weeping and pining until her flesh dried up, her bones turned into rock and all that was left of her was a disembodied voice.

Meanwhile, Narcissus returned home unconcerned and continued to repulse all advances until at last a day came when a young man he had spurned cried out in pain to the gods to grant that Narcissus himself should love and be rejected. The goddess Nemesis heard his prayer and granted his request.

So it was that not long afterwards Narcissus was again separated from his companions during hunting. The day was hot and he was drawn towards a pool of silver-sweet water, cool and clear, untouched by fallen leaves or bracken. The youth lay down and bent his head towards the water intending to drink from it, but was astonished to see the face of a beautiful youth or nymph rise up from the depths as if to kiss him. He drew away, shivering with the shock of this vision. His heart pounding, he bent over the pool again and there the face was, looking up at him. He reached down and, as he thought, was about to touch its lips, but felt only the cold water on his mouth. He gazed enraptured, saw his love gaze back, then raised his arm; the vision's arm raised too. He plunged his arm into the pool, only to scatter his dream again. He knelt then and, with his arms outstretched, pleaded with the surrounding trees to pity him, for he was parted from the face he loved by such a slender margin – merely a film of water. So he pined, lying beside the water night and day, not caring for food or sleep. There disembodied Echo found him and stayed with him, repeating his moans of sorrow and the last notes of his sobbing and his last farewell.

But even in death, journeying to the Underworld, Narcissus again found his fair love gazing at him from the river Styx, and was again tormented. Meanwhile, his sisters, both naiads and dryads, wept and mourned him, while Echo shared their wailing. Building a funeral pyre they went to fetch his body, but it had disappeared. Instead, they found a little flower, shivering on a slender stalk, white petals fringing a circle of gold, bowing to its reflection in the pool.

Commentary

The story of Narcissus has been used extensively as a subject for writers, poets and painters such as Boccaccio, Caravaggio, Rousseau, Poussin, Rilke and even Milton, who used him as the model for his depiction of Eve. His story has also inspired writers such as Paul Valéry and André Gide. Both find a more positive symbolism in the story, Valéry putting forward in his Narcissus poems the value of being inward-looking and self-reflective and Gide arguing in his treatise on Narcissus that only the contemplation of self can lead to knowledge of the truth. Both writers' views make an interesting comparison with the earlier Roman interpretation which saw in the myth of Narcissus a depiction of the supremacy of the soul over the body – a view which greatly influenced Neoplatonic thinking. But arguably the most important appropriation of the myth has been by the psychoanalysts.

NARCISSISM

'Narcissism' is used to describe a psychological state in which a person entertains grandiose ideas of himself to the exclusion of the merits of others. Not only is his main concern and interest directed towards himself, but he is often unable to comprehend or imagine the needs of others. Freud differentiated between two types of narcissism. The first is the pathological one often suffered by schizophrenics who have withdrawn from the external world until they are unable to respect or relate to others, and instead sustain a compensatory sense of their own omnipotence. The second type concerns a normal stage of development of the individual in which the infant sees itself as the centre of the universe and, in this state, subsumes its mother to itself. Freud linked his theory with that of the libido, but other psychoanalysts, such as Eric Fromm (1900–80), see narcissism in a more positive light. For example, this early narcissistic experience can be regarded as vital in providing the instinct for survival or in promoting individual achievement. It is only unhealthy when it becomes obsessive.

Healthy narcissism

Freud argues that narcissism is an originally healthy psychological state out of which the individual develops the capacity to value another as a love object. He maintains that such healthy narcissism is an essential part of normal development. The individual, however, should develop beyond this state and become able to love another person objectively.

Healthy narcissism is connected with self-esteem. All artists, performers and politicians are, to an extent, narcissistic. Indeed, if they did not value their talents, it would be very difficult for anyone else to do so. For, as Fromm convincingly argued, rather than interfering with their art, their narcissism actually helps it. This is because the average person finds the self-confidence of the orator or performer attractive. It could also be argued that, if the artist or performer has real talent, his narcissism is not without foundation.

Self-delusion

If the individual fails to progress beyond the early healthy stages of narcissism, the frustration arising from an inability to love objectively can lead to mental illness. Such arrested narcissism, as the myth shows us, is not love. It is self-delusion which is the opposite of love. Such self-delusion is difficult to detect for it often hides behind a mask of humility and seeming self-sacrifice. It also hides in group ideologies such as nationalism or religious fanaticism in which the inferiority of the individual becomes subsumed into the grandiose status of the collective.

Self-reflection

The strongest interpretations of the myth are based on the assumption that Narcissus is seeing a masculine reflection of himself. For, although in the myth he is seen as rejecting nymphs and youths alike, the emphasis inclines towards homosexuality. This is reinforced by another story in which a spurned youth to whom Narcissus sent a dagger killed himself in front of Narcissus' house, calling on the gods to bring upon Narcissus a similar state of unrequited love. Nemesis answered him and caused the resulting infatuation with his reflection.

There is, however, another version of the myth, mentioned by Pausanias, which states that Narcissus had a twin sister with whom he fell in love. She died at a young age and Narcissus mourned her by looking at his own reflection in the pool. His face being so like hers, he felt as if he were seeing her. His death in this case was caused by grief brought on by bereavement. This account has been dismissed as a rationalization made up by Pausanias. But Pausanias says he has heard it from the Thespian Greeks, though he admits that it was not the most popular account.

If this version is allowed more credence, then a different psychological explanation of the story is possible, which is more in line with Jungian thought. For Narcissus' twin sister can be seen as the feminine aspect of himself. Thus when she is translated into the image in the pool, she becomes a symbol par excellence of the anima. The meaning of the story still concerns a failure of love, but it is the failure to progress beyond the infatuation with the inner feminine that causes it. This, typically, is the stumbling block for many men and is what prevents their being able to achieve a satisfying relationship with a real woman. Narcissus spurns the love of many women, not just Echo, and finds himself locked into the impossible adoration of the woman as idealized image, the woman who is the female counterpart of himself.

Insight

Tiresias' prophecy that Narcissus would only live long if he did not 'know himself' is borne out to some extent by Pausanias' version, for the anima is a part of the self, albeit undeveloped.

ECHO

The original story concerning Echo, a nymph of Mount Helicon, was that she was loved by the god Pan but spurned his love, preferring a satyr. Pan was so enraged that he incited some shepherds to a Dionysian-like frenzy in which they tore her apart. She and Pan, however, are said to have been the parents of Iambe (see Chapter 8). Seen in the context of the story of Narcissus, Echo becomes another image of the anima, an undeveloped feminine presence rather than a separate entity in her own right.

In this respect, a contemporary reading of her would see her betrayal of Hera as a betrayal of matriarchy. Her punishment is therefore a consequence of her behaviour, for it reveals her for what she is – an insubstantial woman who echoes the words of others and has no real opinions of her own.

Insight

It was Ovid who was inspired by the idea of combining the myth of Narcissus with the story of Echo. This has become the most famous version of the myth.

NARCISSUS AS FLOWER-HERO

The poet, writer and mythographer Robert Graves (1895–1985) sees in the story of Narcissus an 'echo' of the annual sacrifice of the spring flower-hero. He compares Narcissus with Antheus, a victim of this ritual who gave his name to others, 'Antheus', or 'flower', being a surname of the Spring Dionysus (see Chapter 1). Graves also compares Narcissus with an image of Orestes with a circlet of lilies round his head, lying in despair beside a pool in which he has vainly attempted to purify himself after the murder of his mother.

THE NARCISSUS AS NARCOTIC

Pausanias records that the narcissus was used together with the lily, hyacinth and crocus to make an unguent. The narcissus itself, as its name suggests, had narcotic properties. In his self-absorption, Narcissus offers an apt image of the adolescent who, unable to connect with the vital springs of life, becomes victim to an alternative, drugged and illusory state. The pining away of Narcissus suggests the kind of death that narcotic addiction induces. The narcissus flower which replaces his body is a powerful symbol of the incorporeality inherent in this condition.

Insight

The name Narcissus comes from the Greek *narkao*, which means 'to deaden'. Narcotics, in general, induce languor and numbness of the senses. In larger doses this can lead to insensibility and death.

KEEP IN MIND...

1 The story of Narcissus is about a youth who spurned women. Instead, he fell in love with his own reflection in a pool, pined away and died.

2 It also concerns Echo, companion of Hera, wife of Zeus. Echo used her gift of entertaining speech to distract Hera when Zeus went off with a group of young nymphs. Hera punished Echo by limiting her speech to copying the last words spoken by another.

3 The story has been used by writers, poets and painters, also by philosophers.

4 Perhaps most important for contemporary times is its use by psychoanalysts, especially Freud.

5 The term 'narcissism' was first coined by Havelock Ellis in 1898. It describes a psychological state in which a person entertains grandiose ideas of himself to the exclusion of the merits of others.

6 Narcissism, as the myth shows, is self-delusion which is the opposite of love. It can be a factor in group ideologies such as nationalism or religious fanaticism.

7 In another version of the myth which has Narcissus falling in love with a twin sister, Narcissus' twin sister can be seen as the feminine aspect of himself – the anima.

8 Echo can be seen as another image of the anima, an immature woman with no real opinions who merely echoes the words of others.

9 The plant narcissus has narcotic properties which can induce drowsiness or, in larger doses, lead to death.

10 Robert Graves sees in the story of Narcissus the theme of the annual sacrifice of the spring flower-hero.

4

Oedipus

Sophocles based his plays *Oedipus Rex* and *Oedipus at Colonus* on the Oedipus myth, and his version has become the canonical one. However, earlier accounts differ in a number of ways. For example versions mentioned by Pausanias make the Sphinx, variously, a piratical commander of a fleet of ships, and a daughter of Laius. The account below is a compromise between Sophocles and Apollodorus, whose more succinct account has Laius himself piercing the child's ankles, and giving the child to a herdsman. Sophocles has the herdsman pass it on to the second herdsman rather than abandoning it on the mountain.

Laius, king of the great city of Thebes, was a powerful and respected man. But, for all his power, his marriage to his queen, Jocasta, was an unhappy one because an oracle had given Laius a terrible warning: if ever he were to have a son, this boy would be the death of him. Accordingly, Laius slept apart from Jocasta – until one night, after feasting, he drunkenly went to her bed. His blood ran hot, and they both cast aside all thought of the oracle in a rush of desire. In due course a son was born, and Laius, fearful of the oracle once more, considered his best course of action. He knew that to kill the child outright would be an offence to the gods, and so instead he persuaded Jocasta that they should expose it on Mount Cithaeron. He gave orders for its ankles to be pierced and pinned together so that it could not even crawl away, and gave it to a herdsman to take to the mountain. Now he felt safe: no infant could survive the ordeal.

That same evening another herdsman pasturing his flocks on the mountain heard a feeble cry mingling with the bleating of his sheep. Following the sound, he came across the helpless infant and immediately took pity on it. Wrapping it in his cloak, he went down the mountain, and lost no time in taking the baby boy to his master, Polybus, king of Corinth. The king and his wife, Periboia, were childless, and so they agreed to regard the boy as a gift of the gods and raise him as their own. They called him Oedipus: 'Swollen Feet'.

As Oedipus grew up, other boys of his age grew jealous of his strength and began to taunt him with rumours they had heard: that he was not in fact the true child of the king and queen. They pointed out, too, that Oedipus was not at all like Polybus in character. The king was known for his mildness, while Oedipus had a fearful temper. Oedipus anxiously questioned the queen, but she would say only that she was his mother and Polybus his father. Still doubtful, Oedipus travelled to the oracle at Delphi, where he asked who his true parents were. The oracle refused to say, but it did give the young man a shocking warning: he should not return to his homeland, for if he did, he would murder his father and sleep with his mother.

Appalled at this news, but still assuming himself to be the true son of the king and queen of Corinth, the young Oedipus resolved never to return there. Instead, he mounted his chariot and lashed his horses on towards Thebes – and, as he thought, away from danger. He had gone no great distance – only as far as Phocis, when the road began to run through a cleft in the mountains. Approaching a narrow place where two other roads joined this one, Oedipus saw a cloud of dust rising ahead and heard the sound of another chariot travelling fast towards him. The two chariots met at the tightest and most awkward place.

'Get out of my way, fool – I have the right of way!' snarled the man gripping the reins of the other chariot. But when Oedipus held his ground, the driver struck at him with a goad to try to force him from the road. Outraged, Oedipus lost his temper, and hit out, both at the driver and his grey-bearded passenger. In a few moments the charioteer lay dead in the dust of the road, along with two other attendants, and the older man's lifeless body hung over the side of the chariot, animated only by the lurching of the wheels on the rutted road as they slowed to a halt. Only one man escaped, fleeing for his life.

Eventually Oedipus arrived in the city of Thebes, intent on starting a new life for himself well away from Corinth. Now the city's old ruler,

Laius, had recently died and been succeeded by Creon, his brother-in-law. Creon had inherited not just the city, but a major problem. The goddess Hera had decided to plague it with the monstrous Sphinx, who had the face of a woman, the feet and tail of a lion, and the wings of a bird. The Sphinx had been taught a riddle by the Muses, and she sat on Mount Phicion and repeated it to the Thebans, carrying off and eating them one at a time when they were unable to solve it. An oracle had told them that they would be rid of this monstrous creature only when someone was able to answer her riddle correctly. King Creon therefore offered the kingdom, and the hand of his sister, Queen Jocasta, to anyone able to achieve this.

Many had tried their wit on the inscrutable Sphinx and failed, but Oedipus was determined to succeed: although fate had made him an outcast from his homeland, yet he would make his mark in Thebes. Approaching the monster where she brooded on Mount Phicion twitching her long tail and restlessly rearranging her great wings, Oedipus demanded that she pose him the riddle.

'What is it,' she began, 'that has but one voice, and that goes on four feet in the morning, on two feet at noon, and on three feet in the evening?'

To her surprise, Oedipus confidently replied, 'Man. He goes on four feet as a baby, and on two feet as an adult. In the evening of his life a stick provides his third foot.'

Completely downcast by this unexpected event, the Sphinx hurled herself in shame from the acropolis and died. The Thebans were overcome with gratitude for the enterprising stranger. Amid rejoicing, Oedipus was crowned king of Thebes, and Jocasta found she had a new husband – one younger and fresher than the old one. In time, she bore four children to this second husband: two sons, Eteocles and Polyneices, and two daughters, Antigone and Ismene.

All seemed well, until a great plague descended upon the city, carrying off the populace even faster than did the Sphinx. As the king, Oedipus felt it was his duty to find out the cause of this affliction and save his adopted people once again. So, for the second time in his life, he set out for the oracle at Delphi, passing on his way through a narrow place where three roads met, and which stirred uncomfortable memories for him. Entering the presence of the god

Apollo at the oracle, he learned the cause of the plague: it would cease only when the murderer of Laius had been killed or banished. Relieved to have at least this much information with which to save Thebes, Oedipus, standing before the oracle, pronounced a solemn curse on whoever had committed the crime, and resolved to track down the unknown man.

Oedipus then sent for the blind seer Tiresias, a man known for his astonishing insight. Reluctantly, the seer came into the royal presence. Knowing that he risked the king's anger, the old man attempted to make him understand the awful truth: 'You yourself have polluted Thebes. You are the self-same man you seek.'

Oedipus was furious at the suggestion that he, who had always done his best for Thebes, could be responsible for its present plight. He refused to accept that there could be any truth in the old man's words, and looked elsewhere for the source of the people's sickness. He even accused his brother-in-law Creon of conspiring against him with Tiresias, in a bid for the throne. But that night, still unsettled, and with apprehension in his heart, he spoke to Jocasta, mother of his four children.

'Jocasta, wife, tell me: when and where did your first husband meet his end?'

'A short time before you came to our city. It was near Delphi. He was murdered by a hot-tempered man, at a narrow place where three roads met in a mountain cleft.'

Oedipus turned away, a sickening horror beginning to grow in him. Then, going quickly from Jocasta's chamber, he sent for the one known living witness of Laius' death, a bondservant who had asked to be allowed to leave Thebes, and who had lived far out in the countryside ever since. Meanwhile, more news was on its way. A messenger came to the palace and announced that Polybus of Corinth had died; Oedipus was invited to his funeral. Though the death of a father was sad news for Oedipus, for a short time it gave him hope: if Polybus really was his father, there was no need to fear the old prophecy now. But the man who brought the news was no ordinary messenger: he was the herdsman who had so many years ago rescued an infant on Mount Cithaeron and taken it to Polybus.

The full story was now beginning to reveal itself. Oedipus now knew that Polybus was not his father, yet he could not be sure who was.

Had Tiresias been right? Could such an abomination really have occurred?

One day Oedipus summoned his wife. They met under a cloudless sky, in the palace courtyard. 'Jocasta,' he began, 'I have a terrible fear. I must discover the identity of my true father. Is there anything you can tell …'

But Jocasta, hands to her mouth, stifling a cry, rushed inside. She had guessed the awful truth for herself.

Within moments the surviving witness, Laius' old servant, arrived at the palace and was led to its master, who was pacing the courtyard. Oedipus stopped and beckoned the old servant, whose fear showed in his downcast gaze and reluctant tread. Then Oedipus, with his characteristically forthright nature, commanded the man.

'Describe to me the man who killed your master.'

'My lord,' the man answered, after a pause, 'I stand before that man.'

At that moment a great wailing came from within the palace. Oedipus hardly heard it. Then a waiting woman to the queen ran from the palace and fell at Oedipus' feet, her face in her hands. Oedipus, as if in a dream, stepped out of the light into the palace. Forcing open a chamber door, he found the body of Jocasta, hanging from a beam. His howl of horror, pain and realization echoing through the palace, he drew his sword and hacked wildly at the silk scarf tied around her throat. The body fell in a heap. Through a window the sun glinted on the gold pins that fastened the robe. Snatching these pins from their folds, and falling heavily to his knees, Oedipus looked for the last time at the mother of his children, as he drove the long pins deep into his eyes. He had been blind to the truth, but now at last he could see.

Commentary

The Oedipus myth is best known for Freud's use of it in his formulation of the 'Oedipus complex'. However, before we look at this and at other psychological views of the myth, it is worth considering the more obvious ways in which the story of Oedipus resembles that of other heroes. His heroic stature tends to be forgotten when he is seen primarily as a model for psychological dysfunction.

Oedipus does not achieve feats of physical prowess in the manner of Heracles or Theseus, but he does save Thebes from the all-devouring Sphinx, and this, in worldly terms, is his great achievement. He shares the obscure parentage that is a feature of many heroes (such as Perseus, or the Celtic Maeldun, or the figure of the 'orphan boy' in Native American myths). He is also a tragic hero in that he bears his suffering patiently, and has elements of the sacrificial victim. The piercing of his feet or ankles is reminiscent of the Norse Baldur and of Christ crucified. He also seems to be singled out by fate in a particularly ironic way, leaving the country where he is actually safe from the prophecy that he will kill his father, unaware that the man he regards as his father has adopted him.

Insight

The Oedipus myth is evidence of a strong belief in predetermination. Perseus, similarly, has no desire to kill his grandfather Aegisthus, yet does so because the old man tries to escape his prophesied fate, ironically bringing about what he is trying to avoid. It seems that, in the Greek view, fate was inescapable, even though individual choice was in some sense possible.

The myth contains a strong symbol of fate in the image of the crossroads. This represents a coming together of factors, and of individual lives. It also implies choice, which paradoxically is still part of this fateful world-view. The narrow cleft seems to funnel the two men towards an unavoidable meeting, and may even represent the birth canal down which the unborn individual travels towards the fateful moment of birth.

We see in the motif of the unknown father a metaphor for the individual's search for identity. The hero must find where he comes from. He must also find and confront the father in order to separate from the mother. It is part of his individuation. In the misguided attempt to cheat fate, we see the Greek insistence on predetermination, and on the individual's subordination to divine will. At the same time, the hero is particularly subject to fate, as he has the particular attention of the gods. There is also an inevitability in the way that the young hero, or god, supplants the old. Cronus provides another example of the old god, and the story of his overthrow by Zeus illustrates the underlying theme (see Chapter 2).

THE FREUDIAN VIEW

Freud first referred to the Oedipus complex in a letter written in 1897, while he was considering his relationship with his own father, recently deceased. The theory he developed was that the child, at about the age of four, becomes sexually attached to its opposite-sex parent and correspondingly jealous of, and antagonistic towards, its same-sex parent. In normal development this phase ends at about the age of seven, as the child begins to identify with its same-sex parent. Abnormally, the child remains fixated in the Oedipal phase. In adulthood the repression of these socially unacceptable incestuous and murderous desires results in neurosis.

Freud at first applied this theory to both sexes. Later he limited the term 'Oedipus complex' to the mother-fixated son, and linked the female counterpart to Electra, who in another Greek myth encourages her brother Orestes to kill their mother, Clytemnestra. This is in revenge for Clytemnestra's murder of their father Agamemnon (her husband), which she has accomplished with the help of her lover, Aegisthus. This myth has much in common with the myth of Oedipus, particularly since Orestes kills the 'false father' Aegisthus as well. Most commentators on Freud have focused on the son–mother relationship rather than that between the father and daughter.

Freud regarded the widespread appeal of the Oedipus myth as evidence supporting his theory. In his view, Oedipus does exactly what the four-year-old boy wants to do: he kills his father and has sex with his mother. Other mythical heroes are less direct;

Perseus and Orestes, for example, kill negative father-figures. So, too, does Shakespeare's Hamlet, who kills Claudius, the man who has murdered Old Hamlet and married Hamlet's mother. In the Freudian view, Hamlet's procrastination in taking his revenge is due to his Oedipal problems. He cannot bring himself to kill a man for achieving his own unconscious desires. Interestingly, the play derives from a Danish legend recounted by the twelfth-century Saxo Grammaticus, itself derived from an older legend – perhaps an instance of the 'Oedipal' theme occurring outside of Greek myth.

BACHOFEN AND FROMM

While many psychologists and commentators on myth agree with Freud that there is a basic antagonism between father and son, there is less support for the idea of the son's incestuous desires for his mother. The psychologist Erich Fromm, in *The Forgotten Language*, acknowledges Freud's contribution to the understanding of myth, but draws on the work of the anthropologist J. J. Bachofen (1815–87) to produce a very different interpretation of the Oedipus myth. In Fromm's view, it is essentially about the conflict between matriarchal and patriarchal power.

Fromm points out that, in older versions of the myth, it is usually predicted only that Laius will be killed by his son – not that the son will marry his mother, Jocasta. Moreover, no extant version mentions Oedipus having any desire for Jocasta. She is simply 'part of the package' that he wins by freeing Thebes from the Sphinx: Jocasta goes with the kingdom.

Insight

If the Oedipus myth were primarily about incest one might expect Oedipus to desire Jocasta and kill her husband in order to have her for himself, but in fact he marries her merely because it is expected of him as the new king.

Moreover, in versions before Sophocles, for example Homer's, while Oedipus does kill his father and accidentally marry his own mother, he discovers his error before he and Jocasta have children; she kills herself, and he goes on to marry Euryganeia. He has his four children by this second wife, continues to rule Thebes, and eventually dies in battle – his death being marked by the elaborate funeral games due to a hero.

Fromm's interpretation relies on Bachofen's view that human sexual relations were originally promiscuous within a small tribal group. This meant that no one knew who a child's father was, while there could be no doubt about the mother. This brought about a system of matrilineal descent, found in many tribal peoples worldwide, including those of pre-twentieth-century North America. This situation gave motherhood, and women in general, a great status. For some reason, however, circumstances changed; sexual relations became more or less monogamous, or at least polygamous. Now a man knew which children were his: the rule of patriarchy had begun.

How this change came about is debatable. Leonard Shlain, in *The Alphabet versus the Goddess*, argues persuasively that the invention of alphabets, and the move from oral to literate cultures, caused a shift towards logical, left-brain, male-oriented thinking. However, the fact that in most cultures, including patriarchal ones, until recently only a minority of people were literate raises doubts about this. Another possibility is that as farming became more efficient, and societies grew more sophisticated, people for the first time had a surplus of goods. Increased materialism made men want to hand on their wealth to their own children, not to the whole tribe.

Whatever is the case, there is evidence that matriarchal societies were at one time more widespread. Fromm cites the myth of Orestes as being about a last struggle between the old forces of matriarchy and the new patriarchy. Aeschylus' Oresteian trilogy of plays puts the two on trial. Orestes is bound by the new code to avenge his father's death; however, according to the old matriarchal code, to kill his mother would be a greater crime than to leave his father unavenged. He kills her anyway, and the Eumenides, or Furies, bay for his blood. However, in the end, with the patronage of the new-order Olympian goddess Athene, Orestes is acquitted.

The Eumenides also enter into the Oedipus myth. In Sophocles' play *Oedipus at Colonus*, the sequel to *Oedipus Rex* (which tells Oedipus' story up to his self-blinding), Oedipus goes to Athens and takes refuge in the sacred grove of these goddesses. The grove is his last resting place. This is just one of several factors which, Fromm argues, link Oedipus to matriarchy. For example, Eteonos, the only city in Boeotia with a cult shrine to Oedipus, also has a shrine to Demeter. Another important factor is his association with the Sphinx. Her riddle is not, after all, so very difficult – especially considering that the Sphinx has become synonymous with inscrutability! Fromm argues that we must apply the principles of dream interpretation to this part of the story, examining the apparently incidental features to find the true meaning. It is not the riddle that is important, or its explanation, but the fact that the answer is 'Man':

> *He who knows that the most important answer man can give to the most difficult question with which he is confronted is* **man himself** *can save mankind.*

This, according to Fromm, represents a basic matriarchal principle – the importance of all humanity. Other principles of matriarchy and patriarchy are compared below:

Matriarchy	Patriarchy
blood ties, the 'law of nature'	man-made laws
feeling	rationality
passive acceptance of nature	efforts to change, control or exploit nature
acceptance of humanity	judgement
unconditional love	conditional love
happiness	obedience
unity	hierarchy

Fromm's view is that all higher civilization, including ideals of universal peace and 'the brotherhood of man', stems from the unconditional love that a mother gives to all her children alike. To a mother, nothing can be more important than her children. Therefore Jocasta's great crime is to put the life of her husband (to whom she is not related by blood) before that of her child. This part of the myth, however, is confused by the fact that different versions ascribe different degrees of involvement to her.

In *Oedipus at Colonus*, Jocasta's brother, Creon, emerges as the enemy both of Oedipus and of the matriarchal principle. He champions rigid adherence to man-made laws and hierarchies, and protests that 'disobedience is the worst of all evils'. Even more pointedly he insists that men must never allow women to get the better of them, and that it is better to fall from power by a man's hand than to be thought weaker than a woman.

Lastly, as Fromm points out, all three Theban plays contain the theme of father–son conflict. Oedipus rebels, albeit unwittingly, against the patriarchal and hierarchical principle represented by his father, but in his blindness he turns against his own sons and has nothing but good to say about his daughters. In the third play, when Creon becomes king of Thebes, his son Haemon rebels against his cruel despotism, and tries to kill his father, committing suicide when he fails. There is certainly a strong case for seeing the incest element of the myth as being, originally at least, of only secondary importance.

KEEP IN MIND...

1 The main source for the myth of Oedipus is Sophocles. Apollodorus is an important secondary source.

2 King Laius of Thebes had been told that, if he had a son, the boy would cause his death, so he slept apart from his wife, Jocasta, until one drunken night he slept with her.

3 Jocasta bore a son, but Laius ordered the boy to be left to die on Mount Cithaeron, his ankles pinned together. However, a shepherd found him and gave him to the childless King Polybus and Queen Periboia of Corinth, who brought him up as their own son.

4 Oedipus eventually came to doubt whether Polybus and Periboia were his parents, and sought the truth at the Delphic oracle, which only warned him not to go home, for fear of murdering his father and sleeping with his mother.

5 To avoid this fate, Oedipus resolved never to return to Corinth. On his way to Thebes he got into an altercation with another chariot driver and killed both him and his passenger – Laius.

6 In Thebes, Oedipus solved the riddle of the Sphinx, thus saving the city from her ravages and becoming its king. He therefore married the old king's widow, Jocasta – his own mother. When the truth emerged, Jocasta committed suicide and Oedipus blinded himself.

7 Oedipus has much in common with other heroes: his strength and intelligence; his uncertain parentage; and a fatal flaw – his anger. The piercing of his feet or ankles is also echoed in some other heroic tales.

8 Oedipus' heroic journey is to find and confront his father in order to separate from his mother – though actually he marries her. The myth could also be seen in terms of spring overcoming winter.

9 Freud saw the myth as representing a phase in infant development in which some children become fixed, failing to separate from their mother.

10 For Fromm, the myth reflected a struggle between promiscuous matriarchy, when paternity was uncertain, and an emerging patriarchy. Jocasta's crime was to put her husband before her child. Fromm regarded the incest element as less important than the father–son clash.

The birth and heroic deeds of Perseus

Hesiod mentions the story of Perseus in his *Theogony* while *The Shield of Heracles*, ascribed to Hesiod by Apollonius of Rhodes, vividly describes Perseus fleeing from Medusa's sisters 'at full stretch'. Quite a full account is given in Apollodorus. This describes Danaë as being shut in an underground chamber, not a tower, but also mentions other accounts in which she is seduced by her uncle, Proetus, not Zeus – which may well have been the case in any real-life story from which the myth developed. The account below is based on those of Apollodorus and Ovid. Ovid, rather inventively, has Perseus relate the Medusa episode in 'flashback' at the feast following his rescue of Andromeda.

There were two royal brothers, twins, who hated each other so much that they fought even while still in their mother's womb. These brothers were called Acrisius and Proetus, and they were the sons of Abas, king of Argos. When their father died, the brothers contested the throne, until in the end Acrisius overcame Proetus and took his father's place. However, Acrisius' rule was blighted by one thing. Although he and his wife, Eurydice, were blessed with a beautiful daughter, Danaë, Acrisius had no son and heir. Therefore he asked an oracle how he might get a son, but was told only that a son of Danaë – his grandson – would one day kill him.

To avoid this fate, Acrisius had a brazen chamber made beneath the ground – though some say it was a high tower – and he shut the weeping Danaë in there so that no man could ever gain access to her and cause her to conceive a child. Yet all-seeing Zeus saw the lovely maiden through the chamber's strong walls, and burned with passion for her. To reach her, to overcome her modesty, and to protect her from seeing a god in his full splendour, Zeus came to her as a shower of gold, pouring miraculously through a skylight. The maiden became pregnant with the child of Zeus. This child was Perseus.

Acrisius was furious to discover that his daughter was with child – and afraid for his own life. Refusing to believe that she had been visited by great Zeus, he shut her in a strong wooden chest and had her cast upon the sea, thinking to be rid of both mother and child. The chest was tossed upon the waves for days, and carried by the currents eastwards, until off the coast of Seriphos it was caught up in the fishing nets of Dictys, brother of that island's ruler, Polydectes.

The kindly Dictys gave Danaë and young Perseus a home on Seriphos, and Perseus grew to manhood. By now the less kindly Polydectes had fallen in love with Danaë, but found that the presence of Perseus seriously interfered with his wooing. So he pretended to be enamoured of Hippodamia, daughter of the Pisan king, Oenomaus, and to be collecting contributions towards a wedding gift for her. Perseus, full of youthful bravado, declared that he would fetch the head of the only mortal Gorgon, the dreaded Medusa. From other men Polydectes required horses, but from Perseus he demanded that he should make good his boast. He knew that anyone who glimpsed a Gorgon would be instantly turned to stone.

However, Polydectes did not reckon with divine intervention. Perseus was favoured by Hermes, messenger of the gods, and by the warrior goddess Athene. Under their guidance, Perseus sought out the three Graeae, who had been old women since birth, and who were the sisters and guardians of the Gorgons. The Graeae shared one eye and one tooth, which Perseus deftly snatched as the sisters passed them round. Now obliged to help him – or remain blind and toothless, the sisters led him to some nymphs who gave him the winged sandals of Hermes, the cap of darkness belonging to Hades – which made its wearer invisible – and a bag in which to put Medusa's head. Hermes himself provided an adamantine scimitar with which to hack off the head, and Athene a shining bronze shield.

Perseus set out alone, wearing the sandals and cap, carrying the bag, and armed with the flashing sword and bright shield. He travelled far, over rough hillsides and through ruined woods. Eventually, as he approached the land of the Gorgons, he saw on the road, and in the fields beside him, silent and statue-like, the petrified forms of unfortunate men and beasts whose last earthly sight had been Medusa's face.

When he arrived the three Gorgons were asleep. Their horrible heads, cloaked in dragon scales and tusked like wild boars, hung heavy. Their brazen hands lay still, their golden wings folded. Summoning his courage, Perseus began to approach stealthily, walking backwards, guided only by the reflection in his shining shield. Then as he stood over them, Athene guided his hand, and with a broad and powerful backward sweep of his arm he brought down the scimitar of Hermes in a flashing arc, severing the serpent-haired head of Medusa. In that instant, from the monster's neck sprang the beautiful winged horse Pegasus and his human-shaped brother, Chrysaor. Perseus took hold of the head without looking at it, stowed it safely in the bag, and made his getaway.

Figure 5.1 Medusa depicted on a vase (note the snake border)

Clutching the bag, Perseus now set off for his home on the island of Seriphos, carried swiftly through the air by the winged sandals of Hermes. As he hovered over Libya, the blood from the grisly head fell in drops onto the desert sand, turning to snakes. The warring winds then carried him this way and that. Three times he passed the constellations of the Great and Little Bear in the north, and Cancer in the south. Buffeted and distrusting night, he touched down on the westernmost shores of the world, near those seas which welcome the weary horses of the sun at day's end.

This was the kingdom of Atlas, a giant of huge proportions. This colossus owned vast flocks of sheep and herds of horses, as well as trees bearing both leaves and apples of glittering gold. Here came Perseus seeking rest and a bed for the night. But Atlas remembered an oracle telling him that one day a son of Zeus would despoil him of his golden fruit. For fear of this calamity the giant had walled his orchard round and posted a huge dragon to stand guard.

Suspicious of the stranger, the giant cried, 'Leave now, or you will never live to enjoy the stolen glory of your invented deeds!' When gentle persuasion failed, Perseus decided to try his strength in a wrestling match. The two heaved and strained, and the ground shook, but in the end Perseus, exasperated and unable to lift the mighty Atlas from his feet, reached for his bag.

'Since my gratitude will not suffice, accept this gift!' So saying, he produced the horrible head of Medusa from its bag in a flourish, making sure to turn his own head away. The mighty Atlas, like others before him, was turned to stone. He became a mountain holding up the sky for evermore.

The winds were now locked up and the sun shone fair on Perseus as he set off again. He passed over many nations, until he came to the land of Ethiopia, ruled by King Cepheus, whose wife was the beautiful but vain Cassiopeia. This woman had angered the Nereids by boasting of her beauty, and they had called on Poseidon to flood the land and send a sea monster to devour its people. Now the only solution open to Cepheus was to offer his daughter Andromeda – as beautiful as her mother, but more modest – to the merciless fangs of the sea monster.

When Perseus caught sight of Andromeda she was fastened to a cliff overlooking the sea. He would have thought her a marble statue had a wisp of her hair not caught in the breeze. So entranced was he that he almost forgot to carry on hovering in the air.

The young woman's parents stood by distraught, but their hopes were raised when Perseus presented himself to them: 'I am Perseus, son of Zeus who came to my mother as a golden shower. I have vanquished the snake-headed Gorgon and ridden the winds of heaven. I propose that, if with the help of the gods I rescue your daughter, she shall be mine.'

Needless to say, Cepheus and Cassiopeia accepted these terms, and Perseus quickly turned to face the monster, which now surged towards its intended prey like a swift galley breasting the waves, its body breaking the water's surface in huge undulating coils. The hero flew up and hovered above, and the beast at once attacked his shadow on the water, taking it for the man himself. Then, like an eagle that grasps a venomous snake close to its head to avoid its deadly bite, Perseus attacked the creature's back. He drove his scimitar through the leathery hide, and the beast arched high in a frenzy, plunged down and then up again, snapping its fangs at the attacker. Winged Perseus evaded the deadly jaws, and stabbed hard through the monster's barnacled ribcage. The hero's wings were now so bloody that he doubted their ability to hold him in the air. But, bracing himself on a rock, he thrust his blade into the creature's groin again and again, until it lay dead.

A cheer rang out from all who watched. Andromeda was set free and Perseus washed off the blood and brine. Next, he built three altars and sacrificed a cow to Athene, a calf to Hermes, and a bull to mighty Zeus. Only when he had given thanks to the gods in this way did he take Andromeda in his arms and make her his wife.

Andromeda bore noble children to Perseus, but not before Perseus had been obliged to fight Cepheus' brother Phineus, to whom Andromeda had been betrothed before being offered to the sea monster. In this fight, once again the head of Medusa was the final arbiter: Phineus and his followers were turned to stone.

Returning at last to his adopted homeland of Seriphos, Perseus found that his mother Danaë and her benefactor Dictys had both fled to the altars for refuge from the violence of the wicked Polydectes, whose desire for Danaë had turned to bitterness. When Polydectes had sent Perseus on the mission to bring back Medusa's head, he had never anticipated that the young man would succeed, so now he was in for a shock. Perseus entered the palace, where Polydectes had gathered his friends, and once again produced the ghastly head from its bag. The persecutor and his supporters were turned to stone.

Perseus made Dictys king of Seriphos and gave the winged sandals, the cap of invisibility, and the bag to Hermes. The head of Medusa, however, he presented to Pallas Athene, to place at the centre of her shield. Now Perseus hurried with his wife and mother to Argos, the land of his birth, anxious to meet Acrisius. But the old man had heard that Perseus was on his way. Fearing that the oracle foretelling his death at the hands of Danaë's son was about to be proved true, he fled to the Pelasgian land. But as fate would have it, the king of Larissa was holding athletic games in honour of his father, and here Perseus came in order to compete, not knowing that Acrisius was in the crowd. Perseus hurled a discus with his usual force, and of all men it struck Acrisius, who died instantly.

Acrisius' divinely foretold fate was fulfilled, and Perseus had little reason other than kinship to regret the old man's death. Nevertheless, Perseus felt ashamed to inherit the kingdom in this way. Therefore he entered into an agreement with King Megapenthes of Tiryns, and the two men exchanged kingdoms. Megapenthes thereafter ruled over the Argives, and Perseus over the Tirynians.

Commentary

The rich symbolism of this complex myth is echoed in myths worldwide: the divinely fathered infant surviving against the odds, and against the wishes of a destructive father-figure; the hero cast upon the ocean and 'born again'; the 'wicked stepfather'; the dangerous quest fulfilled with divine assistance; the wresting of divine fruit from a possessive giant; the reward of the maiden rescued from a monster; the overthrow of the evil king; and the inescapability of fate. Perseus is a very Greek hero in that his virtue lies not merely in physical strength and courage, but in intelligence and astute use of whatever assistance is on offer.

DIVINITY MADE MORTAL

The story of Perseus grows out of conflict. As with many myths, we have brothers who are sworn enemies, like night and day. This dynamic creates an energy which in narrative terms Perseus inherits. We also see in Acrisius the first negative father-figure in the myth. He is the life-denier who tries to prevent the rise of the new generation. In this respect, he is like Uranus stuffing his children back into the earth. He is even more like Cronus, swallowing his children because it has been predicted that one of them will overthrow him. Anthropologically, Acrisius represents the old king's attempts to avoid being supplanted. Psychologically, he represents the possessive father, determined to keep his daughter to himself. Danaë is denied expression of her sexuality, either literally by her father, or psychically by her own superego.

Insight

Seen in terms of the individual psyche, Acrisius represents the ego that locks up the unconscious in a futile attempt at self-preservation, at the expense of life and growth, but which is overcome by the Self, or the divine, in the shape of Zeus.

Zeus here makes one of his many transformations, which indicate the limitless creativity of the divine. The idea that mortals will be destroyed, or at least terrified, by undisguised divinity is found in the Bible and in other myths. When Krishna reveals himself to his friend Arjuna, the latter begs the god to resume his former shape. The pattern of the god impregnating the virgin is also found in many cultures, and includes the visitation of Mary by the Holy Ghost. Danaë's virginity is reinforced by the literal impregnability that Acrisius hopes to secure by locking her in the womblike chamber or, in the other version, the phallic tower.

CAST UPON THE SEA

When Acrisius finds that Danaë is pregnant he could simply kill her. But perhaps this would incur the wrath of the gods. Laius faces a similar problem when his wife bears him a son, Oedipus (see Chapter 4). Both kings try to ensure the infant's death without taking the blame. Acrisius puts mother and son in a chest, which reminds us of the basket in which the baby Moses is placed, and the sarcophagus in which Seth sends his brother Osiris floating down the Nile. Similar symbolism of rebirth into a new consciousness is found in the biblical Jonah, and the Native American hero Raven, who are both trapped in, and then escape from, whales.

Insight

The chest is both womb and tomb, and represents a spiritual rebirth. Perseus, like some other heroes, is thus twice-born. The symbolism is particularly strong in that he is cast on the sea, itself a feminine symbol of potential (as in the primal waters of Genesis) and of the unconscious.

In Dictys and Polydectes we see two more father-figures. Together they make up two faces of the father: Dictys the protective and sustaining, and Polydectes the dangerous, jealous and destructive. Polydectes is a male version of the fairy-tale archetype of the 'wicked stepmother'. True, he does not actually become Perseus' stepfather, but he does want Danaë to become his wife. An anthropological point worth making here is that in many animal species, when a new dominant male takes over and appropriates a female, he kills her immature offspring, thus ensuring the dominance of his genes. There may be a hint of this at work in the case of Polydectes. In another sense, he reflects infantile fear of the jealous, destructive aspect of the father, who threatens to interfere with the infant's monopoly of the mother, and to punish the infant for claiming it (see Chapter 4).

TAKING UP THE QUEST

Polydectes may be the 'wicked stepfather', but he serves an essential function that appears in many hero myths: he sends the hero off on his first test. He does not need to have the hero's interests at heart; in fact, he usually hopes that the hero will fail and die. This is the case when Pelias sends Jason to fetch the Golden Fleece (see Chapter 10). Celtic examples include the giant Ysbaddaden, who sends Cwllwch off on a dangerous quest for magical objects, the securing of which will win Cwllwch the hand of the giant's daughter Olwen, as well as causing the giant's death. The one who sends the hero off, then, has an ambiguous role. He is a force for destruction, and yet he arranges the hero's initiation.

Perseus, like Jason, plays some part in setting up the test. It is his bravado that makes him offer to fetch Medusa's head. Yet in a hero this is a sign of courage rather than foolhardiness, and so Athene and Hermes – his half-siblings – come to his aid. Hermes, messenger of the gods, is associated with the intellect and with communication. The scimitar he presents to Perseus represents intellectual discernment, and the ability to separate from the mother, necessary for individuation. The shield given by Athene is a feminine symbol, protective and reflective. Perseus cannot succeed by force alone: he needs sensitive receptivity in order to accomplish the task.

In fact, other feminine help is also needed. Although some sources give the three Graeae individual names (Enyo, Pemphredo and Deino), they are really one goddess, which is why they share an eye and a tooth. The fact that they appear as a triplicity suggests that, like the Eumenides (the Furies), they are from a pre-Olympian, goddess-based pantheon. Although they are sometimes depicted in ancient art as young and beautiful, they seem closer to the archetype of the Goddess as hag, particularly since their role is to tell Perseus where to find the nymphs – who represent the Goddess in her maiden aspect.

The folk motif of the hero being given three magical objects occurs worldwide. On one level, it encourages us to make good use of whatever 'God-given' gifts we have. The cap of darkness may represent the need for the hero to be self-effacing, lest he be devoured by the monster of his own ego, while the winged sandals of Hermes suggest the power of thought. The bag, a feminine symbol, may seem relatively unimportant, but in fact it is vital: without a container for the head of Medusa, Perseus himself will be petrified, even though its owner is dead. This is a variation on the same theme of divinity being too much for mortals to bear that we find when Zeus transforms himself at the beginning of the story – though Medusa represents divinity in its destructive aspect.

Perseus succeeds heroically in his quest, but only with Athene's guidance. In other words, he has to draw on the positive, sustaining anima figure to overcome the negative, destructive one. His backward approach to Medusa, which avoids looking at her, is the opposite of the normal headlong heroic confrontation; in fact, he succeeds, literally, by avoiding confrontation. Note, too, that he takes Medusa's head, and that it keeps all of its destructive power, though now held within the bag – the containing aspect of the feminine. This is reminiscent of cults of the head found all over the ancient world; for example in Celtic myth the head of Bran has protective and prophetic powers.

In some versions of the story the remaining two Gorgons pursue the hero. Joseph Campbell refers to this motif as the 'magical flight' and explains it in terms of the hero keeping his ego, or sense of self, intact in the face of potentially overwhelming divine power. Perseus is not yet ready for loss of ego and reabsorption into the divine. In Ovid's *Metamorphoses*, Medusa herself was formally a beautiful mortal woman, changed into a Gorgon by Athene when she slept with Poseidon. This is further proof of the danger posed to the unprepared mortal by direct contact with godhead. On the other hand, the beheading of Medusa does bring two noble offspring into the world – Pegasus and Chrysaor.

THE ORCHARD OF ATLAS – A LAND OF THE BLESSED

The domain of Atlas resembles the Celtic Land of the Blessed. It exists in the west, where the sun (a symbol of the hero) sinks, and it is therefore associated with the afterlife. Atlas himself represents the ego, grown to monstrous size, and he jealously prevents access to the fruits of the unconscious. In this, he is something like the God of the Garden of Eden, with its forbidden fruit. In fact, in both cases 'apples' may be taken to refer to fruit in a more general sense. (A Jewish tradition identifies Eve's 'apple' as a fig.)

Perseus wrestles with Atlas, or with the ego, in order to obtain the fruits of the unconscious, but wisely realizing that he must again resort to divine female aid, he produces Medusa's head from the bag. Atlas is left holding up the world, like the ego supporting the structure of the world as we perceive it.

THE MAIDEN AND THE MONSTER

The best-known episode in the myth is Andromeda's rescue, perhaps because Ovid's account focuses on it. The wide appeal of the 'hero rescues maiden from monster' motif is shown by its occurrence in folk tales worldwide, by its adoption in the Arthurian romances, and even by its survival in cinema, for example in *King Kong*. It may also be the prototype of the story of St George and the Dragon. Another example is found in the Hopi tale in which Son of Light rescues his wife from Man-Eagle.

In some versions, and certainly in modern embodiments of the motif, the maiden plays some part in her own rescue. In the story of Perseus, however, Andromeda is entirely passive. Indeed, her stillness as she waits for the monster could be seen as lifelessness rather than simple courage. It takes the positive animus, in Perseus, to bring her to life, to free her from her parents, and to unlock her sexuality. One could see this as feminine initiation. For Perseus, however, Andromeda is the positive counterpart to the destructive female energy represented by Medusa. He cannot form a proper relationship with the feminine, by marrying Andromeda, until he has dealt with the destructive anima, or negative feminine (see also Chapter 11).

The monster sent by the sea god Poseidon is a product of the unconscious, which holds destructive terrors as well as treasures. It has been seen as another negative anima figure, the devouring aspect of the mother, and this may be appropriate, since Poseidon sends it, together with a flood, to punish Andromeda's mother Cassiopeia for claiming to be more beautiful than the Nereids (sea nymphs).

Insight

The sea monster could also represent the lower, devouring aspect of sexuality, which Perseus has to conquer before he can have a true relationship with the female. Certainly in later, Christian-influenced forms of the tale, such as the Arthurian romances, the monster takes on this meaning.

THE HERO'S RETURN

Perseus, having proved himself by achieving the task, now faces Polydectes himself. This confrontation represents the new king replacing the old, and spring replacing winter. But it is also a final rescue – of Perseus's own mother Danaë and the kindly Dictys, the positive father-figure, from the tyrannical Polydectes. Now that Perseus has completed the heroic task of individuation from his parent figures, he can relate in a healthy way to his real mother and the protective father-figure. The rescue, and the placing of Dictys on the throne, represent a rehabilitation of the parent figures in the psyche of Perseus.

As for Acrisius, he is left trying to avoid his destiny. Perseus has no conscious knowledge that his discus will kill Acrisius, but the accident does give him a blameless revenge for the way in which he and his mother were treated by Acrisius. It also kills off the life-denying old king and allows the heroic young king to take power.

The exchange of kingdoms is harder to explain. Presumably this rarely happened in ancient times. It could point to a change of consciousness, as when Pwll exchanges kingdoms with Arawn, Lord of Annwn, the Celtic Underworld, in the Welsh *Mabinogion*.

KEEP IN MIND...

1 Acrisius was told by an oracle that he would be killed by his grandson. To avoid this he imprisoned his daughter Danaë. Zeus, however, came to her as a shower of gold, and she became pregnant with Perseus.

2 Acrisius shut Danaë in a wooden chest and had her cast onto the sea, but Dictys, brother of Polydectes, king of Seriphos, caught it in his fishing nets and took in the mother and child.

3 Perseus grew up, and Polydectes fell in love with Danaë. But he wanted to get rid of Perseus, so he sent him on a mission to fetch the head of Medusa.

4 With help from Hermes and Athene, Perseus killed Medusa, cut off her head and set out for Seriphos, using the head to turn Atlas to stone on the way. He then rescued Andromeda from a monster and won her in marriage, before killing Polydectes and making Dictys king.

5 The original prediction was fulfilled when Perseus accidentally killed Acrisius with a discus.

6 The motifs of a divinely fathered infant surviving against the odds, defeating a wicked stepfather, and rescuing a maiden, are found in myths worldwide.

7 Acrisius is a negative, life-denying father-figure. He represents the ego that locks up the unconscious in a futile attempt at self-preservation. Danaë's rescue is a symbol of rebirth. The sea on which the chest floats represents the unconscious.

8 Polydectes symbolizes the negative, threatening aspect of the father. Yet he also has the role of sending Perseus off on the quest by which he proves himself.

9 Hermes' gift of a scimitar represents intellectual discernment, Athene's shield protection and receptivity. Perseus succeeds only by drawing on the positive, sustaining anima figure (Athene) to overcome the negative, destructive one (Medusa).

10 Andromeda is a passive form of the anima that needs Perseus' animus to come to life. Perseus overcomes the negative anima in the form of the sea monster.

Theseus and the Minotaur

There are several versions of this very ancient myth, which may relate to the destruction of Knossos and Minoan civilization in around 1400 BCE. Ovid vividly describes the labyrinth but seems less interested in the killing of the Minotaur. Apollodorus has Theseus killing the Minotaur with his bare fists. Pausanias mentions several variations. The account below is based on all three writers. As king of Athens, Theseus also appears in Sophocles' *Oedipus at Colonus* (see Chapter 4).

Theseus was one of the greatest sons of Athens – and yet he was born elsewhere, across the sea. His mother was Aethra, daughter of Pittheus, king of Troezen. The king of Athens, Aegeus, had visited Troezen on his way back from the oracle at Delphi, which he had consulted about his childlessness. Pittheus, wanting to be grandfather to a future king of Athens, got his guest drunk and induced him to sleep with his daughter Aethra. In the morning Aegeus left for Athens. But before he did, he hid a sword and a pair of sandals beneath a rock, telling Aethra that, should she bear a son, and if the boy was one day able to recover these tokens from under the rock, he should bring them to Athens and seek his father. However, it is said that Aethra received a second visitor that night, as Aegeus lay in wine-sodden sleep – the sea god Poseidon – and that the god was the true father of Theseus.

Theseus grew up showing many signs of greatness to come. In time, he lifted the rock and regained his human father's sword and sandals, and set out for Athens, choosing the long and dangerous land route, and defeating many foes along the way. Periphetes, whose habit was to beat travellers to death with a bronze club, was just the first.

Theseus tore the club from its owner's grasp and cracked his skull open with it. The club thereafter became Theseus' special emblem, a reminder of his first trial of strength.

When Theseus finally arrived in Athens, Aegeus, of course, failed to recognize this son whom he had never seen before. His new wife, Medea, however, recognized the young man at once through her powers of sorcery, and was immediately jealous of him. Revealing nothing about the youth's identity, she contrived to turn her husband against him. As a result, Aegeus sent him on a mission that could result only in death. It was to capture and kill the Marathonian Bull, a creature then ravaging Attica. The expedition did result in death – the death of the savage bull, which Theseus drove bellowing through the streets of Athens before cutting its throat in sacrifice to the god Apollo. Thwarted in her attempts to destroy Theseus, Medea tried to poison him at a feast, but at the last minute Aegeus recognized his own sword, still carried by Theseus, and dashed the cup from his hand. The father found a son, the son a father, and Medea was forced to flee.

Though distressed by Medea's treachery, Aegeus was delighted to have a son at last, and such a fine one, whose heroic reputation travelled before him. He set about getting to know Theseus – little knowing how short a time he had in which to do so.

Athens at that time was subject to a great sorrow and indignity. Some years previously it had been at war with Crete, whose king, great Minos, son of Zeus, had been determined to avenge the alleged murder of his son Androgeus by the Athenians. He had launched the might of his navy against Athens. Not only this, it seemed that the gods themselves had turned against Athens. Heralded by a blotting out of the sun, plague afflicted the land, leading first to the death of animals, and then progressing to humans. An oracle revealed that, to be spared more suffering, Athens must give Minos whatever recompense for his son's murder he demanded.

What Minos demanded was a tribute whose bitterness for the Athenians would take the edge from his own bitterness at the loss of his son. They were to send him, every nine years, seven young men and seven maidens to be fed to the Minotaur. This monstrous beast was the creation of a broken promise and a shameful deed. To win over the people, Minos had prayed to Poseidon to send a white bull from the sea, promising to sacrifice it to the god. Poseidon obliged, but Minos could not resist keeping such a magnificent beast for himself, and so he sacrificed a substitute. The angry god afflicted Minos' queen, Pasiphaë, with a passion for the animal, so that with the help of the ingenious Daedalus she disguised herself as a cow and persuaded the bull to mount her. The resulting offspring was a monstrous creature, human from the neck down, but with the head of a bull.

Now the young hero Theseus had been with his human father Aegeus just long enough to make himself indispensable, and for his father to rejoice daily that Medea had not got her way. However, the time was approaching for the Athenians to make their third tribute to Minos, to feed the bloodlust of the Minotaur. Despite Theseus' popularity, the people of Athens began to complain among themselves. Every nine years the city state lost the flower of its youth, since Minos insisted on the noblest. Why should Aegeus be exempt?

Sensitive to these murmurings and loyally desiring to defend the reputation of his new-found father, Theseus made his decision. 'Father,' he announced, 'I want to be part of the Cretan tribute this year.'

'Part of the tribute!' exclaimed Aegeus. 'You're my only son, the heir to the throne. Let others go. There's no need for you to go. I forbid it.'

Nevertheless, the complaints continued, especially when the lots were drawn up from which the fourteen young people would be chosen, and when the great urn was brought out in which the lots were always placed.

At last, Theseus confronted his father. 'My dear father,' he said, 'am I not your own son, who vanquished club-wielding Periphetes? Did I not treat that bandit Sinis to the same trick with which he had killed so many, tying them between two down-bent pines and tearing them asunder? Am I not he who hunted down the wild sow of Crommyon, and who outwitted evil Sciron and hurled him into the giant sea-turtle's waiting jaws? And did I not pin Procrustes to his own bed, where he had beaten and lopped so many unfortunates to size? Trust, then, that I will deal likewise with this misshapen creature, and return safely having freed Athens from this grievous obligation.'

His determined appeals beat steadily against his father's reluctance, like Poseidon's waves against a rocky headland. But in the end Aegeus gave his permission. He had just one request: 'Theseus,' he said gravely, 'you may never return from this attempt, though I admit it is a noble one. Should the gods grant you success, do this for me. Before you come within sight of Athens, have the pilot of your ship replace its billowing black sail with a white one which I shall supply, so that I may know you have survived the Minotaur, offspring of the white bull of Poseidon.'

Theseus willingly agreed to this request, and confidently began to prepare for the voyage.

The lots were drawn and some of the noblest and fairest of the Athenian youth, seven young men and seven young women, began their farewells to tearful parents. This time there was some hope that they might return, though it seemed a slim one, since no one had ever returned before.

Theseus himself led his thirteen companions from the Prytaneum – the city's great hall where the lots had been drawn, and went to the Delphinium, where he dedicated to Apollo his suppliant's badge, a branch from the sacred olive tree, bound with white wool. He made his vows and prayers, then went down to the sea and boarded the waiting ship. Aegeus, standing grave-faced at the head of the crowd on the quayside, raised his hand once and let it fall. The pilot's orders rang out amid the cries of gulls and the impatient jostling of the waves on the ship's oak timbers, the oarsmen struck out, and the crew raised the creaking rigging. Soon, to the fourteen chosen ones on board, the yearning friends and relatives onshore were mere specks. The black-sailed ship began to beat its way south across the wine-dark sea towards Crete.

Two days later the ship arrived at Knossos, where King Minos had his palace. The king came down to the water's edge to inspect the young Athenians. He had heard that among them was Theseus, young but already renowned. It was clear to Minos immediately which one he was. The Athenian hero was strong and handsome, of course, but he also had about him an air of almost godlike assurance. Minos thought sadly of his own son, once handsome and strong, and he turned away.

Now, the Cretans had organized funeral games in honour of the king's long-dead son. The Athenians were to be entertained, though held captive, for the duration of the games, and then fed to the Minotaur. Minos now had a sense of apprehension about these games. The favourite to carry away the highest prizes was a man whose bullish name, Taurus, matched his powerful physique. The man's arrogance was hateful to Minos, as were the rumours of his over-familiarity with Queen Pasiphaë – who had already shown her liking for bulls. Therefore, when Theseus asked for permission to compete in the games before being fed to the Minotaur, to everyone's surprise Minos agreed. He secretly hoped that Theseus would get the better of Taurus.

It was customary for the Cretan women to watch the games, and so it was that the king's daughter Ariadne was in the cheering crowd that watched appreciatively as the Athenian hero shamed the overbearing Taurus into second place. Unknown to her father, she fell in love with the young man's godlike form, his courage and his confidence, and she determined to help him escape the clutches of her half-brother the Minotaur, even if it meant betraying her father. She knew that the man-beast was confined in a vast labyrinth of complex design. Its architect was the Athenian exile Daedalus, and he had conceived it with a thousand twists, blind alleys and puzzles of perspective to confuse and disorientate anyone who tried to find a way out of it. Its dark passages were said to wander this way and that, turning back on themselves like a sleeping serpent, or like the river Maeander itself. However, she had met Daedalus, and she knew him to be not without compassion.

In secret, and in disguise, Ariadne went to Daedalus and asked for his help. He took pity on the maid, and on his countryman Theseus, and he provided her with a clew – a ball of thread – to give to Theseus so that once he had found and killed the Minotaur he would be able to retrace his footsteps. He also told her how to find the concealed entrance to the labyrinth. That night she went to Theseus, telling the guard that she wished to congratulate the champion of the games. The young man was delighted to meet this beautiful young woman, whose determination appeared to be something like his own. She, for her part, was no less enamoured of him at close quarters than from afar.

After overpowering the guard, Theseus allowed Ariadne to lead him, under the cloak of night, to the hidden entrance of the labyrinth.

Here she gave him the oil lamp which normally stood by her bedside, as well as the all-important ball of thread. One end of the thread he fastened to the inside of the door. A glance of promise passed between them, then he was swallowed up by the darkness, and Ariadne was left to wait in hope and apprehension with only the stars for company and consolation.

Theseus walked softly, the ball of thread over his wrist unravelling silently as he trod. The air smelt stale and slightly damp. The passage led gently downwards. After a while it divided and he took the right fork. A little way further and again he had to choose. Sometimes there were chambers that seemed huge at first but then turned out to be small. At other times he entered caverns that really were enormous, but where there was no way on, and where even the way by which he had entered would have been hard to find without the thin thread stretching before him. At each division of the passage he listened, and looked for signs that the monster had passed this way. Sometimes he heard the drip of water, sometimes the pulsing of his own blood. So he continued for hour after hour, until he began to wonder if the Minotaur was not an invention of men's minds.

Then he saw a scrap of red Athenian cloth, and then another. Then bones, the pitiable remains of former tributes. Then as he paused and listened at another crossroads he heard, far off, a bellowing, savage but seeming to speak of lonely suffering. He took the path in that direction, and the bellowing came closer. Now, too, there was a rank animal smell on the air, and more human remains on the ground.

The bellowing had stopped. Only an occasional snort guided him. The Minotaur seemed restless, hungry for its nine-yearly feast and sensing that it was due. Shielding the lamplight with his cloak, Theseus stealthily approached a twist in the passage, beyond which he expected to meet his enemy. He was not disappointed. At the last moment he threw off his cloak and stepped forward. The flaring yellow lamplight revealed a hideous sight: the huge figure of the Minotaur, with its filthy but powerful human limbs, thick neck leading to the swaying bull head, and large, startled eyes that were now focused on the intruder.

Theseus threw down what was left of his ball of thread, and in that same moment the creature lowered its head and charged. With no time to draw his sword, Theseus stepped adroitly to one side. The

Figure 6.1 Theseus killing the Minotaur

creature hurtled past, sending the lamp guttering to the floor. In the darkness, hot, reeking animal breath mingled with the smell of lamp oil. The creature bellowed in anger and launched itself at Theseus. The hero's strong arms found those of the Minotaur and the pair grappled, this way and that, across the chamber, the Minotaur's nails digging into the man's arms. At last, Theseus found himself astride the man-beast, drew his sword, and plunged it into the thick, bullish throat, bringing the Minotaur's miserable life to an end.

In the fight they had rolled who knows where across the earthen floor, and Theseus was now faced with a new problem. Where was the ball of thread Ariadne had given him? He groped carefully across the floor, feeling for it. At last he had it, and he began to follow it back, winding it up as he went.

Hours later he arrived at the entrance and embraced the faithful Ariadne. It was nearly dawn, the time when the Athenian youths would be fetched and taken to the labyrinth. This time, however, there was to be no sad procession to the hidden entrance. Theseus broke into the rooms where his fellow Athenians were held, and led them quickly to the waiting ship, accompanied by Ariadne. He paused only to stove in the bottoms of the Cretan ships before setting sail for his adopted homeland.

Now this tale might have a happy ending, and there are those who say that it did. Indeed, Theseus and Ariadne deserved it. However, most agree that on the return journey Theseus ordered their ship to dock at the island of Naxos, a safe distance from Crete. Here, Ariadne, perhaps pregnant with Theseus' child and suffering from seasickness, was abducted by the god Dionysus, with whom she was later to have children. Those less charitable say that Theseus abandoned her for a maiden who had taken his fancy on the voyage to Crete.

Whatever was the case, as the ship eventually approached Athens, Theseus was sufficiently distracted – perhaps by grief for his lost Ariadne – to make a fatal error. He forgot to order the black sail to be changed for the white one given to him by Aegeus to use as a signal. The old man, looking out to sea from the Acropolis, saw the black sail, despaired, and threw himself from the cliffs to his death. Theseus' homecoming mingled tears of joy with tears of sorrow. He was now king of Athens, but at a great price.

Commentary

This rich myth based on a legendary ruler of Athens, and possibly on an actual ruler of Crete, is widely known thanks to its compelling imagery: the apparently doomed young men and women, the bull-man in the labyrinth, the maiden with her thread, and, of course, the hero himself. But Theseus established his credentials as an archetypal hero long before his journey to Knossos.

A HERO IN THE MAKING

The early life of Theseus bears all the typical marks of the hero. Like so many heroes-to-be, his paternity is obscure, and he sets off on what Joseph Campbell calls the hero's 'road of trials' to find his father, proving himself on the way. His first trial, in itself an initiation into manhood, is to move the boulder and retrieve his father's sword and sandals.

> **Insight**
>
> Like the young Arthur, Theseus must remove the sword from the stone, the incisive phallic symbol from the female earth element, separating himself from the mother.

Theseus is now ready to 'step into his father's shoes'. Taking the long, dangerous route to Athens enables him to prove his strength, cunning and courage by pitting himself against the various ogres he meets on the way. They are symbols of the life-denying aspect of the ego, negative faces of the as yet unknown father who is the goal of the quest.

When Theseus gets to Athens he has to tackle the negative anima in the form of Medea, a woman who has already demonstrated her dark powers and capacity for ruthlessness (see Chapter 10). In some versions she tries to seduce the young man and turns against him when he rejects her, which, in Freudian terms, suggests that he overcomes Oedipal desires (see Chapter 4). In other versions she is simply the 'wicked stepmother' who resents her husband's offspring by another woman. In many myths the hero's first encounter with the father is perilous, and here that danger is projected onto Medea, although it is Aegeus who nearly kills Theseus.

> **Insight**
>
> It is typical of the hero myth that Theseus is sent out on a dangerous mission by a father-figure. The test for Theseus – overcoming the Marathonian Bull – also makes a link between him and bulls which is developed in the story of the Minotaur.

MINOS AND PASIPHAË

The name 'Minos' seems to have been a generic term for the ruler of Crete during Minoan times, rather like 'Pharaoh' in Egypt. Sir James Frazer says that the Minoan kings had to have their kingship reaffirmed every eight years, and that Minos would go at the end of each term of office to commune with his father Zeus in a cave and have his rule for that period appraised. If he was found lacking, he might be replaced by a younger man. This would explain why Minos needed to ask Poseidon to send a bull in order to persuade the people of his continued powers, particularly as bulls often symbolize virility. Frazer links Minos with a bronze man, Talos, said to have been given to the king's mother, Europa, by Zeus, or in another version by Hephaestus directly to Minos (see Chapter 11). By one account Talos was a bull, and Frazer suggests that he and the Minotaur were one and the same, and represented royal solar power. The tribute of youths and maidens may also relate to this eight-year cycle of royal office. Ovid says the tribute occurred every nine years, Frazer every eight. Certainly, it is plausible that human sacrifice might be regarded as a way to renew the king's solar power.

Joseph Campbell, in *The Hero with a Thousand Faces*, describes Minos as a great man who chooses to inflate his own ego by increasing his possessions, rather than honour the spirit by keeping his part of the bargain with Poseidon. The price he pays is that his wife has intercourse with a bull, and that he is saddled with the monstrous offspring. It may also be that by making a second-rate sacrifice he fails to receive the gift of virility that the correct one would bestow, and so Pasiphaë couples with the animal itself. It should be added in her defence that she is keeping up a family tradition: Minos himself was born to Europa after she was seduced and abducted by Zeus – in the form of a bull.

THE MINOTAUR AND THE LABYRINTH

At the start of the twentieth century the archaeologist Sir Arthur Evans carried out excavations at Knossos and discovered the remains of a great palace-complex covering several acres of land. Its design involves a maze-like complexity of passages and irregularly shaped halls, which may be the origins of the mythical labyrinth. One prominent find was a room containing a throne carved out of a single piece of alabaster. Near this room was a large collection of ceremonial double-headed axes, or *labrys*. The word 'labyrinth' in fact means 'house of the double-headed axe'. There was also strong evidence for a bull cult: remains of a life-size bull fresco; a golden bull mask, probably worn in ritual; and a fresco and pottery apparently depicting an occasionally fatal 'bull-leaping'. Bull-shaped *rhytons*, vessels used to pour ritual libations, were also found.

The Minotaur ('Bull [*taurus*] of Minos) may have had historical origins in an actual bull cult, and its killing may represent bull sacrifice. But, as a symbol, the Minotaur is, of course, more than just a bull. He is a monstrous mismatch of man and beast, representing the bestial in man. We can compare Theseus' entry into the labyrinth with heroic descents into the Underworld, representing the unconscious. Theseus is hunting down, confronting and killing the monster of bestiality lurking in his own mind – although, to a modern mind, it is probably the confrontation rather than the killing that is important.

On another level, the Minotaur has been seen both as a masculine and feminine symbol. Adrian Bailey, in *Caves of the Sun*, expands on the solar connection made by Frazer, linking the myth to the sun's seasonal 'death' when it descends into its cave, which brings fertilizing rains, followed by a rebirth. He describes the Minotaur depicted on a coin with ears of corn sprouting from its tail, like the bull of Mithras (the Roman solar god derived from Zoroastrianism), and adds: 'Thus the true purpose of the myth is revealed: the goddess through her agent strikes the great solar bull in its cave. The labyrinth is the cave of the sun.' By this thinking, Ariadne is a virgin goddess, and Theseus is her agent.

Whereas Bailey sees the bull as a masculine, solar symbol, Joseph Campbell, in *The Power of Myth*, describes it as a symbol of the moon, and therefore (paradoxically) of the feminine. This is because the horns of the bull resemble the crescent moon, creating an image of the goddess astride of the masculine, as the horns sit on top of the bull's head. To Campbell, the sun (associated with the lion) symbolizes eternity as something which transcends time, while the moon, with its ever-repeating cycle, symbolizes 'eternity within the field of time'.

There are other reasons to associate the Minotaur with the feminine. The image of the masculine hero penetrating the dark and winding labyrinth does powerfully suggest the male principle penetrating the forbidding mysteries of the feminine, to confront the negative anima in the form of an archaic personification of the Great Mother devouring her children.

Insight

The word *labyrus* is related to *labia*, giving support to the idea that the labyrinth is feminine, and that in entering it Theseus is penetrating the womb of the earth. Historically, this may represent the up-and-coming state of Athens confronting the decadent matriarchal cult of the older civilization.

ARIADNE AND HER THREAD

Ariadne is a representative of the virgin goddess. In this, she resembles Pallas Athene helping Perseus to kill Medusa. Campbell likens Ariadne to other goddess figures who take it upon themselves to protect and inspire the hero, from Dante's Beatrice to the Virgin Mary. Because Ariadne is a woman, she is able to assist Theseus' passage into and back out of the feminine. She also represents the positive anima, with which the hero is able to make a relationship after he has confronted the negative anima or devouring mother.

The thread itself is full of symbolism. It has been linked to the breath of life linking the human being to the cosmos. It is also the fine line of connection between the conscious and unconscious mind, and between the body and soul. In the Upanishads it links this world to the divine world; the Sanskrit word for thread, *sutra*, also means a teaching. For Theseus, it fulfils something like the function that Inanna's messenger performs for her when she descends into the Underworld (see Chapter 9). Antony Stevens identifies it as a particularly feminine symbol, due to women's age-old connection with weaving, and indeed it is what enables Theseus to return to the virgin goddess, in the shape of Ariadne.

Insight

According to Stevens, 'The thread may be understood as an archetypal symbol of the life principle stretching through time as a means of conscious orientation and a guide to understanding.'

The role of Daedalus is interesting. Campbell describes him as a kind of 'hero as scientist' for whom thought leads to truth and liberation. However, we might also see him as representing a danger: the power of the mind not properly linked to conscience. He constructs the model bull that enables Pasiphaë to satisfy her bestial passion. Moreover, he designs the labyrinth as well as giving Ariadne the means of finding a way out of it. He seems more concerned with *how* a thing might be done than with whether it *should* be done.

THE RETURN

It is part of the archetypal pattern that the hero returns to his people, and Theseus returns to become a notable king of Athens. One might think it strange that in the best-known versions of the myth he abandons Ariadne, but if one thinks of her as a goddess, perhaps this is necessary for his survival; in which case, her marriage to Dionysus is more fitting. In Greek myth goddesses very rarely have sexual relations with mortal men, and certainly never marry them; while women seem to survive unions with gods, a man who couples with a goddess is in peril of his life.

It also seems, on the face of it, an unfortunate oversight that Theseus forgets to change his sails, thus killing his father. Apollodorus neatly explains this by having Ariadne carried off by Dionysus, so that Theseus is too preoccupied with his grief to remember about changing the sails. But again, on a higher level, it may be necessary for Aegeus to die. The young hero-son must supplant the old king in order to regenerate the kingdom. In some other myths, the father-figure sends the hero on the near-impossible mission, and then is killed by the hero on his return. Aegeus may not send Theseus to Crete (though in some versions Aegeus bows to pressure from his people), but it must be remembered that Aegeus has previously sent Theseus after the Marathonian Bull, and then nearly poisoned him. One begins to wonder if the young hero's failure to change the sails really was an oversight, or whether it is just an ethically acceptable way of stepping, at last, into his father's shoes.

KEEP IN MIND...

1 Theseus was the son of the Aegeus, king of Athens, who drunkenly slept with Aethra when away from home. He left a sword and a pair of sandals beneath a rock, saying that, if Aethra bore a son who could one day recover them, he should seek out his father.

2 Theseus removed the sword and sandals, and travelled to Athens, proving his strength and courage by defeating several foes on the way.

3 Aegeus' wife Medea turned Aegeus against this unidentified youth, so Aegeus sent him to kill the Marathonian Bull. Theseus succeeded, but was almost poisoned by Medea before Aegeus recognized his own sword, and saved him.

4 Athens was obliged to give a tribute of seven youths and seven maidens to Minos every nine years to be fed to the Minotaur in the labyrinth. Theseus insisted on being part of the tribute.

5 Equipped with a ball of thread given to him by Ariadne, Theseus entered the labyrinth, killed the Minotaur, and found his way back out. He sailed for Athens with Ariadne, but forgot to change the colour of his sail to tell his father Aegeus that he was alive. Aegeus therefore threw himself off the cliff top.

6 Theseus proves his heroism by passing the father's test, defeating foes – in a sense negative aspects of the father – and finding his father.

7 Medea represents the negative anima, and Ariadne the positive, helpful anima. The bull could be seen as a symbol of virility, of the feminine, or of the bestial in human nature. It could stem from an actual Cretan bull cult.

8 Theseus penetrating the labyrinth suggests the male principle penetrating the forbidding mysteries of the feminine, to confront the negative, devouring anima.

9 The thread has been linked to the breath of life linking humanity to the cosmos, and to the connection between the conscious and unconscious, and between the body and soul.

10 Archetypally, Aegeus has to die to make way for the succession of the young king.

7

Odysseus and the Cyclops

The source for this is, of course, Homer's *Odyssey*, which dates from around 750 BCE. Homer has Odysseus tell the story in the first person, at the request of King Alcinous, the father of Nausicaa. Hesiod in his *Theogony* (c. 700 BCE) mentions the Cyclopes as giving Zeus his weapons of thunder and lightning.

Though long-wandering, far from home, and buffeted by waves and ill fortune, Odysseus had not lost his curiosity, and he desired to see something of the land of the Cyclopes and its inhabitants. He and his men spent the night on a neighbouring island, within earshot of the Cyclopes' voices and the bleating of their flocks. In the morning, leaving the bulk of the fleet moored up, he set out in his own ship, with his crew. They churned the grey water with their strong oars, and before long they could make out a cave entrance near the sea, its high arch overhung with laurels. Outside the cave stood a roughly built yard of stone, pine and oak, and as the men gazed, into this yard strode the huge Cyclops, looking more like a wooded peak than a man.

Odysseus steered his ship in close to the shore, dropped anchor, and then went ashore with the twelve best men in his crew. He took with him a goatskin of some of the finest wine ever tasted, dark and mellow, a gift from a priest of Apollo whose family Odysseus had protected. In addition, he took some food in a leather wallet. He wanted to be prepared, for he had a foreboding about the disposition of the giant whose hospitality they intended to put to the test.

Soon they reached the cave, but its owner was away, tending his fat sheep in the pastures nearby. Inside, there were baskets of cheeses, folds filled with lambs and kids, and well-made vessels brimming with whey. The men were all for making off with some of these and setting sail. Odysseus, however, was determined to meet the owner of the cave. He even had some hope of receiving friendly gifts, despite the Cyclopes' reputation for lawless ferocity. So Odysseus and his men lit a fire, killed a goat, and made their offerings to the gods. Then they settled down to wait.

Eventually, a trembling of the ground around them announced the shepherd's return. He heaved a huge bundle of firewood off his shoulder, and the crash as it hit the ground echoed around the cave, making the men retreat to its darker recesses. From the shadows they could see a monstrous, rough-skinned creature, with a single, saucer-like eye in the middle of his forehead. The Cyclops drove his fat sheep into the wider part of the cave and hauled a huge stone over the entrance. He then sat down and proceeded to milk his ewes in a methodical fashion. Finishing this task, he lit up a fire, and by its flickering light he saw Odysseus and his men for the first time.

'Strangers!' he cried. 'And who might you be? Are you traders, or marauding pirates out for what you can get?'

Standing well out of the shadows, Odysseus addressed him boldly: 'We are Achaeans returning from Troy, and we are proud to say that we belong to the forces of Agamemnon. We visit you as suppliants, hoping that you will entertain us as befits guests. I'm sure you're familiar with the laws of hospitality, and your duty to the gods who protect travellers.'

'Stranger,' answered the Cyclops in a sneering tone, 'you must be a fool or a man who knows little of these parts, to talk to me about duty to the gods. I care nothing for Zeus and his crew, for we Cyclopes are stronger by far. If I spare you, it won't be for fear of them! But tell me, where did you moor your ship? I should love to see her.'

Suspecting the monster's intentions, the wily Odysseus answered, 'My ship was wrecked by Poseidon, who drove us onto your shores. We were lucky to escape with our lives.'

For answer, the ugly brute jumped up, reached out a hairy arm, and snatched up two of the nearest men. Dashing their brains out on the stone floor as if they had been puppies, he ripped them to pieces and greedily made his meal of them. The men were transfixed with horror, even Odysseus. But when the Cyclops had washed down the raw flesh with ewe's milk and lain down to sleep, Odysseus reached for his sword, intending to creep up and stab him to death. Then a thought occurred to him – how would they ever move the huge stone from the cave mouth unaided? So, instead, he and the men resigned themselves to sit and wait for daylight.

When dawn's first flush lit the eastern sky, the Cyclops awoke and carefully milked his ewes. Then he seized two more men for his breakfast and was soon crunching their bones between his teeth. Wiping his mouth with the back of his hand, he stood, rolled aside the stone, and led his flock off to graze, having replaced the stone behind him. Odysseus and his men were left to pray to Athene for their deliverance, and to rack their brains for a way out.

Presently, a desperate scheme came to Odysseus. In a corner of the cave stood a great staff of green olive wood which the one-eyed monster had put aside to use when it was seasoned. To the men it was like the mast of a big ship. Odysseus led the men in hacking off a length of it, as big as five men could comfortably manage. He then directed them to work it to a sharp point, which he then held in the embers of the fire to harden. When it was ready, they hid it under the dung which was scattered all over the cave. Odysseus then directed his companions to cast lots to see which four men would help him plunge the stake into the eye of the Cyclops.

The day passed slowly, Odysseus trying to keep up the men's spirits with thoughts of revenge and home. At last evening came, and the Cyclops returned with his sheep and goats, shepherding them all into the cave for safekeeping for the night. He milked his ewes, made up a fire, and once again feasted on the flesh of two unfortunate men.

Odysseus knew that now was the time to hatch his bold plan. He poured out a bowl of the fine wine which he had brought with him and carefully preserved. Stepping up to the monster, he addressed him: 'Cyclops – have some wine to wash down your meal. We brought it for you as a friendly gift, little expecting this savage treatment. But how can you expect to have human visitors ever again after the way you have behaved?'

The Cyclops, unabashed, took the bowl and drained it. The delicious vintage gave him such pleasure that he asked Odysseus for another bowlful, adding, 'And do tell me your name, so that I can make you a valuable gift in return.'

Three times Odysseus refilled the bowl, and three times the Cyclops drank it off. Finally, as the brute swayed drunkenly over the men, Odysseus addressed him in a tone of politeness: 'Cyclops, you wish to know my name, and I will tell it to you. In return, I would appreciate the gift you promised me. My name is Nobody. That is what everyone calls me.'

'In that case,' slurred the Cyclops, 'of all his men, I will eat Nobody last. That's your gift!' Then, smiling twistedly at his own wit, he swayed, and crashed onto the floor of the cave, starting to snore even while vomiting a bloody mess of wine and human flesh. Odysseus signalled to the four men, and together they held the sharpened pole into the fire until it was about to burst into flame. Now pulling it out they charged at the sleeping Cyclops and thrust the red-hot sharpened point into his single eye. The flesh sizzled, and Odysseus used his weight to twist the stake home. Blood spurted all around, and the Cyclops let out an unearthly bellow.

Hearing his cries of pain, the other Cyclopes quickly gathered outside the cave. 'What's the matter, Polyphemus?' they asked anxiously. 'Is someone trying to kill you?'

'Nobody is trying to kill me!' groaned the Cyclops. 'Nobody's treachery is doing me to death!'

'In that case,' they said, relieved, 'you must just be ill. Pray to your father Poseidon to cure you.' At that they went away.

Still moaning, the great brute pulled the boulder from the cave mouth. He then sat down in the entrance and stretched out his arms in the hope of catching the men trying to escape. But Odysseus was too clever to be caught in this way. Instead, he told his men to bide their time. Meanwhile, he prayed to Athene and tried to think of a plan. Finally, one came to him. He told his men to round up some of the biggest rams with the thickest black fleeces. Using wiry willow shoots from the monster's bed, they strapped the sheep together in threes. The middle one of each was to carry one man, except that the leader of the flock, a large, muscular ram, was to carry Odysseus alone.

Odysseus and his men passed another sleepless night, praying for dawn. When at last the first light came, they seized their rams, and hung underneath them by clutching the beasts' thick wool. The Cyclops, though worn out by the night's drama, still ran his hand over the back of each sheep as it left the cave, but he failed to notice the men clinging on for dear life underneath! Last to emerge was the ram bearing Odysseus.

'My sweet ram,' sighed Polyphemus, 'why are you the last of the flock today, when usually you proudly lead the way? Are you grieving for your master's eye, gouged out by that Nobody when I was too drunk to defend myself? How I wish I had him in my clutches now!' Then he patted the ram, which then went on his way.

As soon as they were away from the cave, the men quietly slipped down from under the rams, and drove the whole flock towards the ship. The men left waiting were at first overjoyed, but then saddened to hear of the deaths of their comrades. Nevertheless, they positioned themselves at the oars and pulled hard.

When they were still within earshot of the island, Odysseus, elated at their escape, could not resist taunting the Cyclops. 'So, he was not so stupid after all, the man you meant to eat last! Now Zeus and his gods have paid you back for your crimes against hospitality.'

The cheated Cyclops bellowed his fury. Then, groping blindly, he tore off a pinnacle of rock and hurled it in the direction of the taunting voice. It fell just beyond the ship, and the wave washed the ship back towards the island, so that they were nearly beached. When they had managed to get further out, Odysseus declared his intention of giving the Cyclops one last piece of his mind. His crew tried to dissuade him, but to no avail.

'Cyclops, if anyone asks you who took out your eye, tell them that it was Odysseus of Ithaca, son of Laertes, Sacker of Cities.'

The Cyclops groaned again. 'So the prophecy is fulfilled. But I always thought the deed would be done by a great hero, not a puny runt of a human like you.'

Odysseus continued his taunts. 'Not even Poseidon will heal you now!'

At this, the Cyclops lifted his hands to the sky, and prayed in his anguish to his father to curse the wandering Odysseus. And great Poseidon heard his son's prayer. Then the Cyclops picked up another huge rock and hurled it with all his might towards the fleeing ship. It missed by yards, but this time it fell landward of the craft, and washed it on its way towards the rest of the fleet. Odysseus and his men were safe – for the time being.

Commentary

The *Odyssey* is a voyage myth related to a type of Irish myth known as *immrama*, sea-voyage quests. The story of Jason and the Argonauts is another. Some of these myths, including the *Odyssey*, may have their distant origins in these Celtic shamanistic voyages in the realms of the unconscious, but it is also likely that many of the episodes have been brought together from different myths.

THE CHARACTER OF ODYSSEUS

Odysseus is a sophisticated hero in that, while he is strong and courageous, he is also very resourceful. His intelligence and imagination get him and his men out of numerous predicaments. In the Cyclops episode he bears some resemblance to the Trickster figure that occurs in the myths of some cultures, especially the Native American. Homer often describes him as 'wily'. He does seem foolhardy in visiting the Cyclops, and even naive in hoping for generous treatment, but his scheme for getting out of the cave is ingenious. The trick of calling himself 'Nobody' is adroit and amusing.

Insight

Odysseus calling himself Nobody could indicate that he is setting aside his ego, which would fit with his being the last to leave the cave. If so, he certainly gets it back when he boastfully taunts the Cyclops from aboard the ship.

THE CYCLOPS

Polyphemus is a type of the life-denying, voracious ogre who represents both the negative father-figure and the individual locked in the ego. His spiritual stuntedness shows in his lack of respect for the gods; even when he prays to his father Poseidon, it is for revenge. Ogres often have something they tend and value dearly, which the hero threatens to take away. Often it is a daughter, as in the Celtic myth of Cwllwch and Olwen; for Atlas it is his orchards (see Chapter 5); and for Polyphemus it is his sheep, which he treats in a notably tender and civilized fashion compared with his behaviour towards human beings.

The one eye of the Cyclops is mirrored in the 'eye' formed by the cave entrance, which is an opening into the earth. Both suggest a limited perspective – almost literally 'tunnel vision' (unlike the 'third eye', similarly positioned but denoting spiritual vision). However, there is an intriguing geographical explanation. Homer describes the Cyclops as looking like a 'wooded peak' and elsewhere identifies the island as Sicily. A one-eyed giant resembling a mountain, who builds fires in a cave, blocks and unblocks its entrance, emits a stream of hot, lumpy liquid, and then hurls rocks into the sea – this sounds remarkably like that island's dominant peak, the volcano Mount Etna.

THE SOLAR CAVE

Odysseus' entry into the cave is a version of the archetypal heroic descent into the Underworld. On the seasonal level this represents the sun's descent into the 'cave' of winter. The fire burning there is the continued life of the sun, the seed waiting to burst into life. Odysseus takes his twelve best men, representing twelve months of the year. Of these, six are eaten by the Cyclops, who in this context represents winter. Similar symbolism is involved in Persephone having to spend six months of the year in Hades (see Chapter 8).

In a pattern familiar in solar myths, Odysseus and his surviving men are 'resurrected' from the tomb-like cave on the third day, after the stone has been rolled away. The stone closing the entrance is like a solar eclipse, or perhaps another event that blots out the sun, such as a volcanic eruption, though it could also relate to the three dark nights before the new moon.

To complete the solar imagery, the men blind the Cyclops with a stake hardened in his own fire, and then escape under rams. The ram is the astrological symbol of Aries, and therefore of the spring equinox. It may be that here, and in other myths where the ram is a means of escape, the symbolism is of spring rescuing humanity from winter. (See also Chapter 8.)

Insight

Odysseus escapes with six men. If he is the solar hero emerging from the cave of winter, the six men could be seen as the six planets (traditionally including the moon) then known to the Greeks.

KEEP IN MIND...

1 The tale is a famous episode from Homer's *Odyssey*. Odysseus and his men come to the island of the Cyclopes and Odysseus takes twelve of his men ashore, intending to test the hospitality of the inhabitants.

2 Odysseus and his men are trapped in the cave of the one-eyed sheep-rearing Cyclops Polyphemus, who begins to eat the men two at a time.

3 Odysseus and his remaining men secretly sharpen an olive stake to blind the Cyclops. They get him drunk. Odysseus tells him that his name is Nobody.

4 When they manage to blind Polyphemus, he calls to the other Cyclopes for help: 'Nobody is trying to kill me!' They assume that he is just ill and leave him alone.

5 Odysseus and remaining men escape by tying themselves beneath the Cyclops' sheep, but Polyphemus calls on his father Poseidon, cursing Odysseus.

6 Odysseus is a hero who depends on intelligence and, in this case, trickery, rather than brawn. In this story he is something of a Trickster figure.

7 Polyphemus is a type of the life-denying, devouring ogre who represents both the negative father-figure and the ego and guards his treasure – in this case sheep.

8 The myth has solar symbolism. The entrapment in the cave is like a descent into the Underworld.

9 The stone closing the entrance is like a solar eclipse. Each man escapes under a ram, a symbol of the spring equinox, when the sun is in Aries.

10 If Odysseus himself is the solar hero, the six surviving crew could represent the six planets (including the moon) known to the ancient Greeks.

The abduction of Persephone

> This myth is considered to have originated no later than the seventh century BCE. It is found in Hesiod's *Theogony*. But the most famous accounts are in Ovid's *Metamorphoses* and in the Homeric *Hymn to Demeter*.

'We will sing you this ancient story,' said the nine Muses, 'but perhaps you have no time to hear it now.' 'Sing it right through,' said Pallas Athene. Then Calliope, chief of the Muses, rose to her full height, her bright hair flowing. Fingering her lyre with doleful chords, she began half-speaking, half-singing, a hymn of praise to Demeter:

Lady of the crops, the corn, the richly yielding earth,
lady of the golden sword and glorious fruits,
awful goddess who must bless the land and give it laws, or all mankind
  will die,
rich-haired Demeter, who deserves high praise.

Then she began the story of the rape of Demeter's daughter, Persephone. It happened, she said, because of Aphrodite. Aphrodite was beginning to feel that she was losing her power. She was frightened by Hades roaming the earth. But he in turn was frightened by the giant Typhon, who, although bound fast below the island of Sicily, was trying to escape by means of earthquakes and volcanic eruptions. Hades feared that such gapings in the earth would allow too much light into his kingdom and frighten the shades and spirits in his care. In fact, after roaming the earth and satisfying himself that there was no immediate danger, he was about to settle back into his kingdom. But Aphrodite was already alarmed and planning to take action.

She summoned her son Eros and told him that, besides feeling threatened by Hades, she feared that she was losing the power of love over the earth. Those goddesses who had chosen virginity, such as Athene and Artemis, had not helped her cause, and it now seemed that Persephone was also choosing to remain a virgin. In an effort to subdue her two worries at one stroke, she asked Eros to visit Hades and pierce him with an arrow so that he would fall in love with Persephone. Selecting his sharpest arrow, Eros went off to perform this task.

Soon afterwards Persephone was innocently playing with some nymphs in a wooded glade, picking spring flowers. Suddenly, she spotted a new bloom, one she had never seen before. It was rare and beautiful, growing at the edge of the glade, a little apart from the other flowers, so she ran over to get it, thinking to bring this trophy back to show the nymphs. The radiant flower, however, was a deliberate snare, planted by Zeus to help his brother Hades achieve his desire. Zeus was Persephone's father and considered an alliance between his daughter and her uncle would be a beneficial one as it would unite two-thirds of the earth's kingdoms. He knew, though, that Demeter would never consent to such a marriage and so he kept his plan secret from her.

Just as Persephone reached out for the flower, the earth gaped open and Hades emerged in his golden horse-drawn chariot, seized her and made off with her so swiftly that, by the time she cried out, she was far from her companions. Only Hecate, queen of the night, and Helios, the sun god, heard her frightened screams before she plunged down into the Underworld and the earth closed over her.

When Demeter realized her daughter had disappeared, she was distraught. She roamed throughout the world, over land and sea, searching in vain for her. At night she carried pine-torches in her hands so she could continue searching. All the while she neither ate nor slept. At last she came to a little thatched cottage and asked for a drink. When she was drinking, a cheeky boy called out laughingly that she was greedy. The goddess threw the grain drink angrily at the boy and turned him into a newt.

She kept searching for nine days and on the tenth she met Hecate, who came towards her as dawn was breaking with a torch in her hand. 'I heard the cries of your daughter,' said Hecate, 'but do not know where she went.' Then she advised Demeter to consult Helios, son of Hyperion. Together the goddesses flew to the bright sun god. Helios told them that Zeus had given her daughter to Hades, who had taken her down into his gloomy kingdom. 'But', he said, 'do not grieve overmuch, for he is not an entirely unsuitable husband for your daughter.'

Demeter, however, was racked with grief and anger. Refusing to attend the gathering of the gods on Mount Olympus, she wandered in the towns and fields in the guise of an old woman. One day she arrived at Eleusis and sat by a well with her dark veil drawn over her. The three daughters of King Celeus came to the well and took pity on her, inviting her to lodge with them. She accepted their kindness and was entertained at the palace by Celeus' wife, Metaneira, who had unexpectedly given birth in later years and had her new-born baby Demophon on her knee. Observing Demeter's sadness, an old woman, Iambe, began to entertain her with jokes to raise her mood. Iambe had to work hard but eventually she became so lewd and daring, both in speech and gesture, that she finally forced a laugh from the goddess.

Then the king's wife asked Demeter if she would be nurse to her baby. Demeter accepted and every day held Demophon to her breast, pouring ambrosia over him and breathing her life-giving breath on him, while at night she hid him in the heart of the fire. But his mother, being anxious for her child, came down one night and spied on Demeter. When she saw her put the boy in the flames she screamed out in fear. The goddess heard her and snatched the infant from the fire, laying him on the ground. Then she turned on his mother and said angrily: 'How stupid you mortals are! If you had not spied on me and feared for his life, I would have made your son immortal – he would never have known age or death. Now that you have intervened, he cannot escape the Fates and death!'

'But', she added more softly, 'he will retain honour because I have lain him on my knees and nursed him.' Then she stood up and, throwing off her dark veil, revealed herself in her stern beauty. Light shone from her and fragrance wafted from the folds of her robes, filling the house.

Then Metaneira fell down, her knees trembling so violently that she was unable to move or even pick up her crying child. Then Demeter instructed Metaneira and her three daughters to build a temple in her honour in Eleusis, and there to perform the secret rites that she would teach them.

But Demeter still grieved for her daughter and refused to join the other gods on Mount Olympus. Instead, she caused a year of famine. The grain refused to sprout and the ground remained barren. Seeing that all of life was under threat, Zeus sent the lovely young goddess Iris to Demeter's temple to intervene. Iris told Demeter that Zeus was expecting her at the assembly of the gods. She tried to entice her with offers of gifts and new powers, but Demeter would not be moved, vowing that she would not set foot on Mount Olympus, or cause grain to swell again, until she was reunited with her daughter.

At last the stubbornness of the goddess prevailed and Zeus called Hermes and told him to go down into Hades and persuade its dark lord to send Persephone back up into the world. Hermes descended to the kingdom below the earth and found Hades sitting on a couch and Persephone beside him, pale and brooding.

'Dark-haired Ruler of the Land of Shades,' said Hermes, 'I am sent by Zeus to bring back the lovely Persephone so that her mother can see her again. Only in this way can she be persuaded from her dreadful plan to keep the seeds from germinating and causing the death of all the men on earth. Without the race of men, the gods will no longer be honoured. As for Demeter, she has withdrawn in anger to her temple in Eleusis.'

Hades bowed grimly to the request of Zeus and told Persephone to go to her mother, at the same time urging her not to forget him as he was in many ways a suitable husband for her and could offer her great power over his realm.

Then Persephone was filled with a rush of happiness and straightaway climbed into Hades' golden chariot while Hermes took hold of the horses' reins and they prepared to leave. However, just before she went, Hades slipped a seed of pomegranate into her mouth. Then Hermes drove the horses hard and they went swift as the wind, unhindered by mountain, river, rock or valley, until at last they came to Eleusis and drew up outside Demeter's temple.

Immediately she saw her daughter, Demeter rushed out like a madwoman and caught her up in her arms, clasping her tightly. Then a sudden fear came to her.

'Tell me,' she urged, 'in all the time you were in Hades, did you taste or eat any food there?'

Then Persephone said she had eaten nothing since her abduction except that, just as she was leaving, Hades had thrust a pomegranate seed in her mouth which she could not help tasting.

'Then', said Demeter sadly, 'you will have to return to his shadowy realm for a half of each year. But the other half you may spend with me and your father Zeus. And each year, when you emerge above ground again, the flowers will bloom around you and the earth spring into blossom wherever you tread.'

Then Hecate with her bright hair came up and embraced Persephone and after that became her adviser and companion.

Soon afterwards Zeus sent the goddess Rhea for Demeter, who returned with her mother to Mount Olympus. Zeus gave Demeter new powers as a gift from the other gods and confirmed that Persephone might live with her for half of the year. He also asked her not to think too harshly of Hades.

Then Demeter returned swiftly to earth and lifted the curse she had put on it so that the grain grew and the buds sprouted and the land was fruitful again. But before returning to Mount Olympus, she went back to the palace of the king of Eleusis and gave instructions for the secret rites that were to be performed at her temple.

And the Mysteries she taught were of so deep and hidden a nature that no one might find out about them, for the human voice was too awed to speak of them. The fortunate initiate who knows her secrets, however, receives happiness and favour both on earth and after death, unlike the others who know only darkness and gloom.

Then Calliope finished her tale with a last dirge upon the lyre, calling on Demeter and her daughter to give good gifts and cause continued fruitfulness to those on earth.

Commentary

GRAIN-MOTHER

The name 'Demeter' derives from *Da-mater* or *Ga-mater*, meaning Earth Mother. It links with Gaia, the original earth goddess of Greek mythology, who is also Demeter's grandmother. Demeter herself is associated with agriculture and, particularly, with grain. She therefore has a dual role as mother and as fertilizer of the earth. In fact, the two are so closely related that, when she is deprived of her child, the earth is deprived of fruitfulness.

TRIPLE GODDESS

Demeter also has links with the ancient triple-aspected earth goddess revered by the Celts. Traditionally, this early goddess figure possessed three faces, that of the maiden, mother and crone. These, in turn, corresponded to a division of the seasons into spring, summer and winter. Depictions of the goddess would represent her as three figures sitting together who were understood to be her three facets.

Insight

The Greeks saw the introduction of agriculture as synonymous with the advent of civilization. Thus Demeter, having apparently instructed Triptolemus, another king of Eleusis, in the science of farming, was regarded as having laid the foundations for human civilization.

Persephone was also called *Kore* which simply means 'the maid'. As Kore, she carries flowers and accompanies her grain-bearing mother. But, below ground, she changes and becomes the awesome goddess sitting in state with her husband Hades. This change from innocent youth to experienced age occurs annually, and Demeter is part of it, making the earth barren while her daughter is below ground, and being inseparable from her when she is above ground. Between the two of them they make a fair representation of the three aspects of the goddess, but if a third figure is needed, Hecate, who becomes the companion of Persephone, fulfils this role. Originally a youthful, bright-haired goddess, she later became more generally known as a dark sorceress figure linked with the Underworld (see Chapter 1).

HADES, THE REALM OF EXPERIENCE

Hades, or Pluto to the Romans, was given the Underworld as his realm when the earth was divided between himself and his two brothers, with Zeus having the land and Poseidon the sea. He was therefore Zeus' brother, and it was Zeus who tacitly allowed him to seize Persephone. But it is possible to regard Hades as the dark, shadow-side of Zeus. Psychologically, therefore, Persephone is seen to move from the realm of the mother to the realm of the father.

of Persephone

Every girl underwent this separation at her time of marriage. It was the separation between innocence and sexual experience which, to the Greeks, was overtly linked with the fertility of the earth.

The realm of Hades itself, although feared by Persephone, was understood to be a place where treasures or riches could be found. Apart from souls being famously retrieved from it, so also were gifts, such as Youth, which Aphrodite sent Psyche to look for. Hades' Roman name, Pluto, links with *plutus*, meaning 'wealth'. Again, this accords with the idea of the Underworld containing buried treasure. For the Underworld is both the place of decay and the place for the engendering of new growth. It is where the grain hides and gathers its powers before bursting forth with new life. (The Greeks also literally kept their grain underground in jars.)

Insight

The Greeks saw a strong link between women and the earth. Intercourse with a bride was described as 'ploughing a furrow'. Plato famously remarked that, in the matter of childbearing, the earth did not imitate woman; it was woman who imitated the earth.

FOOD AND THE MEANING OF THE POMEGRANATE

The symbolism of tasting food, which forms the irrevocable link between Persephone and the Underworld, is an interesting one. Physical acts such as eating or touching the ground in a new place could magically bind the newcomer to it. For example, touching the ground proved fatal for the Celtic hero Oisin when he returned to Ireland from a magical 'Otherworld'. However, the symbolism of the pomegranate itself is important. It was considered a particularly mystical fruit – so much so that the Greek writer Pausanias was afraid to speak of it. But the Phrygian myth of Attis gives an account of its origins, saying that the pomegranate tree sprang from the castrated male genitalia of Agdistis – a hermaphrodite child of Zeus who later became Cybele. When, subsequently, the nymph Nana plucked a fruit from the tree and put it in her lap (more probably her womb), she immediately became pregnant with the divine child Attis. The pomegranate, therefore, was a symbol of masculine sexuality, probably because of the abundance of its seeds. Thus, when Persephone tastes the pomegranate seeds, she is symbolically submitting to sexual experience, which is why she can never fully return to her innocent state. Because the juice of its berries was thought to resemble blood, the pomegranate was also associated with death and was therefore an appropriate fruit to find in Hades.

IAMBE

The old woman Iambe, who appears in this story as a servant of Celeus and Metaneira and who jested with the sorrowing goddess, has also been identified with Baube or Baubo, a goddess subsequently featured in the Eleusinian Mysteries and who was given a temple at Paros. A version of the story featuring Baubo says that she joked lewdly with Demeter and pulled up her skirts to reveal her buttocks. In some versions, she also reveals a young child in her womb, a laughing boy who is thought to represent Dionysus. Baubo may be indicative of more ancient deities of sexuality. The comic episode of Iambe or Baubo, coming as it does at a moment of tragic feeling, is also suggestive of the two great comic and tragic modes of Greek drama. Iambe herself is supposed to have given her name to iambic metre, so she may at some level represent comic verse drama.

THE WOMEN'S FESTIVALS AND THE ELEUSINIAN MYSTERIES

The myths of the ancient Greeks were closely bound up with their drama and their ritual. The myth of Demeter and Persephone is particularly telling in this respect, because it not only relates how Demeter set up her Mysteries but is itself the subject of them. In fact, the myth of Demeter and Persephone gave rise to a plethora of festivals.

There were three festivals a year which were strictly for the observation of women. Two of them, the Stenia and Thesmophoria, were held in autumn. The Stenia was a nocturnal festival at which the lewd joking of Iambe/Baubo was ritually re-enacted by bantering between the women. It formed a prelude to the Thesmophoria, a three-day festival marking the departure of Persephone and the onset of winter. The Skira, held in early summer, concerned the return of Persephone and the ritual preparation of threshing floors for the processing of grain.

The return of Persephone was also celebrated by both men and women in the Lesser Eleusinia held in February. But the most important festival of all was the Greater Eleusinia, which originally took place every five years, but later became annual. It was held in autumn and lasted for a week. In preparation, the *hiera*, or sacred objects, were taken from the temple of Demeter in Eleusis to the Eleusinion, located at the foot of the Acropolis in Athens. They were processed along the Sacred Way which joined the two cities. Then the initiates were called and prepared by ritual bathing in the sea, together with the sacrificing of piglets. After solemn sacrifices in Athens, on the fifth day a solemn procession took the *hiera* back along the Sacred Way to Eleusis. This procession also featured the mystical child, the young Iacchos, a boy that Persephone was said to have borne to Zeus, and who was associated with Dionysus. As the procession reached the city walls, masked figures mocked it, again recalling the comic episode of Baubo or Iambe.

The central drama of the myth was re-enacted in the sanctuary of Demeter. This was located just inside the city walls of Eleusis and contained the Telesterion, a huge square building capable of accommodating 3,000 people. Also in the sanctuary was the cave of Pluto and the Kallichoron, a sacred well which represented the Well of the Dancing Maidens where Demeter sat and rested when she arrived in the city. Although the content of the central drama is not documented, it was almost certainly based on the theme of Persephone's descent under the earth and her return. Being held at harvest time, it is also believed to have featured the ritual death and resurrection of the goddess in the form of grain. Certainly, the drink that Demeter was given in the myth, composed of water, barley and mint, was drunk during the Eleusinian rites, and may have contained the grain fungus *ergot*, a powerful hallucinogen. The rituals were stated by Homer to be connected with immortality, so a symbolic process of death and rebirth must have occurred culminating in a theophany – the manifestation of a deity.

Insight

The Homeric *Hymn to Demeter* includes the famous words: 'Happy is the man who has seen these mysteries; but for the un-initiate there are no good things for him once he is dead, only darkness and gloom.'

DEMETER'S SYMBOLS

One of Demeter's main emblems was the torch because she used it in her search for Persephone. It is probable, therefore, that torches were used in a ritual procession in darkness, signifying a symbolic death experience. The magical child, Iacchos, or Dionysus, may also be linked with Demeter's attempt to confer immortality on the infant Demophon. In this respect, it is possible that the torches were also used in a ceremony of purification by fire. The sacrifice of the piglets, which took place in Athens, reflected a version of the story in which a herd of pigs descended with Persephone when the ground gaped open. Pigs were considered magical chthonic animals by the Celts as well as by the Greeks.

THE MOTHER ARCHETYPE

Demeter was understood first and foremost in her role as the Great Mother. This is borne out by the fact that statues of her, in her sanctuary at Eleusis and elsewhere, never stand alone. She is always flanked by Persephone, and also sometimes by 'The Mistress'. Although Pausanias was fearful of revealing her name to non-initiates, the Mistress was in fact Despoine, another daughter of Demeter's, fathered by Poseidon who ravished her when she was distressed and seeking Persephone. In Despoine's own temple both she and Demeter were carved out of a single piece of stone by Demosthenes. The presence of 'The Mistress' as well as 'The Maid' underlines the mystery of the Motherhood of Demeter. The fact that both are carved out of the same stone, yet are distinct from each other, denotes the paradoxical separation and homogeny of mother and daughter.

Insight

Although Demeter and Persephone were depicted as separate statues in their Temple at Eleusis, they were often treated as two aspects of the same goddess, one denoting age and the other youth.

The dual image of mother and daughter goes some way towards illustrating Jung's attitude to the Mother archetype. Jung differentiates between the mother archetype and the anima, or inner female figure, who would be more appropriately depicted as the Kore or The Mistress. He sees the Mother as all-encompassing, representing, like the earth itself, fertility, fruitfulness and agriculture as well as deep hollows such as caves and wells. This is her Gaia aspect, in which she is originally unconscious matter, the matrix of potential meaning and symbolism. She is therefore earth, sea, underworld and moon, and her cosmological power inspires awe and devotion.

At the emotional level, the Mother represents sympathy, nourishment, protection and fostering. Hers is the protective magic circle, the mystical mandala and all intuitive and spiritual wisdom. Her dark womb is the mysterious place of transformation and rebirth. Conversely, in her negative aspect, she can become entombing, devouring and witch-like, symbolic of the dark abyss and the gaping grave. Jung records the psychological difficulties experienced by the daughter whose possessive mother refuses to let her go, but beyond this, and especially with reference to the Eleusinian Mysteries, he recognizes the regenerative symbolism in the combined image of mother and child. For, together, the mother and child depict generation and self-renewal. This is true of mother and son, of course, but the combination of mother and daughter has a different potency, because, at one level, the daughter is also her mother. The mother's renewed youth is reflected in the daughter, while the daughter's maturity is imaged by the mother. Together they turn cyclically in time, perpetually maturing and renewing their powers.

In the myth, Persephone is the renewing force without which Demeter is unable to replenish the Earth. The drought is caused not by her stubbornness but by the abduction and rape of Persephone. Demeter's grief at the disappearance of her daughter, although reflected in the barrenness of the land, is not the cause of it. As soon as the earth's barrenness begins to cause death, Zeus realizes that he must reach a compromise with the goddess, for it was his shadow-self that abducted and raped her. Cosmologically, Demeter, too, is forced to compromise, knowing that, in order to be renewed, the earth needs fertilization from the masculine. The resulting agreement, echoed in the pattern of the seasons, demonstrates a proper harmony between the male and female principles. It also allows Persephone the necessary annual release from her mother when she can unite with masculine power in the chthonic realm and experience her own divinity.

Psychologically, the descent into Hades represents the descent into the unconscious. Jung sees the dark cave as being the primordial place where consciousness and unconsciousness can be united. The descent into the depths promises healing, for hidden within it is the jewel of wholeness. Jung speaks of the magic circle or *temenos*, the sacred precinct where the split-off parts of the personality can be united.

All crypts and underground sanctuaries are places where this can be ritually experienced. They are images of the matrix, the powerful womb of the feminine where the union of opposites can issue in new and vigorous life.

As a representative of the Great Mother, Demeter links with other great goddess figures such as Ishtar–Inanna, Cybele, Isis and the Japanese goddess Amaterasu. Isis, in particular, was considered by the Greeks to be her counterpart, and the myths of the two goddesses have many similarities. Isis' sorrowing search for her vanished husband, Osiris, and the attendant barrenness of the land, parallels Demeter's search for Persephone. Then, like Demeter, Isis seeks to bestow immortality on a child by hiding him in a fire and is prevented from doing so. Also, in Isis' own Mysteries, a lewd exposure of nakedness was ritually conducted between two groups of women on barges floating on the Nile, echoing that of Baubo and Iambe in the Greek festivals.

Insight

Whereas the other great mother goddesses are linked to the child as young son, Demeter is primarily identified by her relationship with her daughter Persephone. In this, she offers a unique depiction of the Mother archetype.

KEEP IN MIND...

1 The myth of Persephone begins with the deliberate plot, conceived by Aphrodite and brought about by Zeus and his brother Hades, to make the innocent young Persephone fall through a chasm in the earth into Hades' kingdom below the ground.

2 Persephone's mother, Demeter, knows nothing of this plot and is devastated at the disappearance of her daughter.

3 While grieving for the loss of her daughter, Demeter caused a whole year of famine in the land. The gods of Olympus could not let this continue, so they decided to offer a compromise and allow Persephone to return from Hades.

4 Just before returning, Persephone had eaten a pomegranate seed, given her by Hades. Having eaten his food, she was bound to Hades and had to return to him for half the year, but could now remain above ground for the other half of the year.

5 Demeter lifted her curse of barrenness from the earth. She also established the secret rites that were to be performed at her temple in Eleusis.

6 'Demeter' derives from *Da-mater* or *Ga-mater*, meaning Earth Mother, and links her with Gaia.

7 Hades itself was a place where riches could be found. The god Hades' Roman name, Pluto, comes from *plutus* meaning 'wealth'. The idea of the Underworld containing buried treasure is echoed in the psychological idea that the unconscious contains buried riches which, if retrieved, are beneficial to the health of the psyche.

8 The Greater Eleusinian festival was the most important Greek festival of all. Originally taking place every five years, it later became annual. It was held in autumn and lasted for a whole week. Although its rituals were a close-kept secret, it is thought to have involved a symbolic process of death and rebirth leading to the manifestation of a deity.

9 Demeter links with other great earth goddess figures, particularly Isis, whose sorrowing search for her vanished husband, Osiris, and the consequent barrenness of the land of Egypt, parallels Demeter's search for Persephone.

10 The Eleusinian Mysteries also featured a mystical boy-child whom Persephone was said to have borne to Zeus, and who was associated with Dionysus.

Orpheus and Eurydice

The account below is based on Ovid's *Metamorphoses*, on Apollodorus, and on Virgil's poignant accounts in his short poem 'Culex', and particularly in his *Georgics* – which gives a spellbinding description of the effect that Orpheus' music has on the inhabitants of Hades. Some details are taken from Pausanias.

In ancient times Orpheus ranked among the most gifted of men. When he sang and played upon his lyre, no living thing could fail to be moved by the sweetness of his music. No wonder – his father was said to be great Apollo, the god of music, for whom the infant Hermes had created the first lyre from a tortoise shell. Orpheus' mother was Calliope, 'Lovely Voice', one of the nine Olympian Muses who inspire all true poets and musicians.

Orpheus was one of Jason's Argonauts on the voyage to win the Golden Fleece. No conventional big-muscled, spear-rattling hero, Orpheus made his contribution by soothing the savage waves, as well as the crew. He even saved their lives by singing more sweetly than the Sirens, who would otherwise have lured the men to their deaths on the rocks.

However, Orpheus was not to be duly rewarded for the joy he brought to others with his art. He met his own heart's desire in the beautiful dryad Eurydice, but when he summoned the god of marriage, Hymen, to bless their union, all did not seem well. Hymen appeared in his saffron mantle, but he pronounced no blessing, nor gave any auspicious sign. Even his torch spluttered and smoked, refusing to burn bright and clear.

Soon after the wedding, Eurydice went walking with her sister dryads in a meadow by a river. As they walked and talked, there appeared another son of Apollo, Aristaeus, who was mad with desire for Eurydice. Scorning her recent marriage, he pursued her, while the other dryads scattered in fear. Fleeing through the lush grass, Eurydice failed to notice a viper, which reared up and bit her. The venom spread quickly, too quickly even for Aristaeus to get his way. Soon the young bride was descending to Hades to live a gloomy life among the shades, far from sunlit meadows and far from her sisters, whose sorrowful wailing reached to all the mountain peaks around.

The dryads punished Aristaeus by killing his other great love – his bees. Orpheus, meanwhile, had heard the news. Despairing, he stood on a lonely shore playing such melancholy music that even the waves wept salt tears. Day after day he mourned, until he resolved to seek his love, even in death, and took himself to the gloomy cavern of Taenarus, in the Peloponnese. Here was the entrance to Hades, into whose terrible depths he must descend.

The path that Orpheus trod was long and lonely, its darkness lit only by hope of seeing his love again. Dimly visible spirits brushed his face, cold hands reached greedily to feed on his human warmth. At last he came to the grimly coiling river Styx, shrouded in mist so that no one could see what lay upon its furthest shore. He paid Charon, soothing the ferryman's ill-temper with a few chords of his lyre. The lifeless shades whispered all around, a dry susurration like dead leaves stirring in a breeze. By following the way they seemed to lead, Orpheus found himself approaching the fearful palace of Hades, King of Darkness. Soon, he stood before the skull-decked thrones of dark-faced Hades and his pale-faced queen, Persephone. Invited by a simple gesture to speak his business there, Orpheus began, first stroking the strings of his lyre.

'You great deities, to whom all mortal creatures must return, I come to you not, like audacious Heracles, to capture three-headed Cerberus, but for the sake of my dear wife. I have tried to endure, but my love has conquered me – a thing which surely you must understand, since you too were joined by love. Now, I beg you, reweave the dire fate of my Eurydice, unravelled long before her natural span of years. Grant her the gift of life again, and I assure you that when her true time comes she will own your sovereignty. Grant not this, and I shall never return to light and life, but rather yield you my life too.'

Saying this, he played, and so overwhelmingly lovely was the sound that from the darkest depths of Erebus the ghosts trooped up in awe to listen, settling like flocks of birds roosting in the woods at dusk. The shades of young men killed nobly in battle, of old women who after long lives had left the light, all came to hear. The jaws of Cerberus' three heads dropped open; the wheel of Ixion stood still; Tantalus forgot the torture of his thirst; Sisyphus sat entranced upon his boulder listening. The three Furies shed their first and only tears hearing this sad music. Even the slime-choked river Cocytus and the nine-times-weaving Styx ceased flowing.

Great Hades and Persephone themselves were moved, and summoned Eurydice from among the recently dead. 'Take your bride,' said Hades. 'But be warned: should you once turn to look upon her before you reach the outer world, you will lose her for ever. Think not to win us twice with music and fair words.'

So Orpheus, filled with a tremulous joy which he hardly dared own, led on, across the Styx, and up the mist-hushed passages leading out of Hades. Many times he almost turned to look upon his Eurydice. Hearing nothing but his own breath, many times he wondered if she was indeed behind him, and if he had not been cruelly tricked. At last the darkness grew less thick, and a long ray of light pierced the gloom and played upon the strings of his lyre. So near the world of light and life, his heart leapt, but still feared to find himself alone. To dare his joy, to try his fear, against wisdom, he turned and looked.

But there had been no trick, for there was Eurydice right behind him. Yet at that moment she let out a cry of deep anguish: 'Oh Orpheus, see what you have done! Now I must return to everlasting death. The Fates recall me, and I am bound around with dark night.' And even as her helpless arms stretched out towards her husband, she faded like smoke and was lost to him.

Sick with the awful realization of his folly, and with regret weighing on him as if he had woken to find himself his own wife's murderer, Orpheus retraced his steps along the winding, dark passages in an attempt to regain his lost love. This time he was rebuffed by Charon, and no amount of pleading would move the grim ferryman: there was to be no second chance. Orpheus returned to the world, and for a full seven months he grieved, his lament melting the hearts of tigers and setting groves of oak trees moaning in sympathy. Everywhere he went he mourned Eurydice, although many women would have warmed to his wooing had he not been preoccupied. At last a group of Ciconian women, engaged in wild Dionysiac rites, and perhaps enraged at Orpheus' stubborn fidelity to a dead woman, set upon the stricken lover and tore him to pieces.

The wild women hurled Orpheus' head and harp into the river Hebrus, and rolling mid-current the head still cried out, pitiably, 'Eurydice, Eurydice!', as it was swept swiftly away towards the open sea.

Commentary

Many myths deal with a hero's quest for eternal life, perhaps through drinking from a certain fountain, or eating a particular plant – as when in Babylonian myth Gilgamesh seeks 'the watercress of immortality'. Others involve the hero, or heroine, in a descent into the Underworld, the land of the dead, whether to assert the power of life, to pass a test, or to attempt the restoration of a loved one as in the case of Orpheus. On one level, this myth is simply about bereavement: the horror of loss, and the aching search to breathe life back into the loved one through recollection or art. But it is also a type of the hero's descent into the Underworld.

THE DESCENT

The Sumerian goddess Inanna (whose Babylonian counterpart is Ishtar) descends into the land of the dead, ruled over by her dark sister queen, Ereshkigal, to assert her power, and to attend her brother-in-law's funeral rites – though in a variant of the myth it is to plead for the return of her consort, Dumuzi. Inanna is killed and hung on a meat hook. She is only rescued because she has had the foresight to tell Ninshubur, her messenger, to raise the alarm if she is not back in three days.

Nor is Orpheus the only Greek hero who makes the grim descent. The last of Heracles' twelve labours is to fetch Cerberus, the monstrous, three-headed guard dog of Hades. Theseus goes there in an attempt to abduct Persephone, and only narrowly escapes, while the great hero Odysseus is permitted to visit Hades and talk to the ghosts there. These heroic descents show that the ultimate heroic challenge is to overcome the fear of death. There are also more mystical aspects to this: the solar hero whose descent imitates the daily death and rebirth of the sun; and the descent into winter, from whose dark seed new life springs.

In some cases the descent is made to bring another, or others, back to life. The Christian version of this is Christ's harrowing of hell. There is self-sacrifice, too, in the version of the Inanna myth mentioned above. We also find, in Norse myth, that, when the god of light Balder is killed owing to Loki's trickery, Balder's brother Hermod goes into Hel – the Norse Underworld – to plead for his return. There is a possible link here: Balder is killed by a spear of mistletoe – a powerful plant which is the only thing anywhere that can harm him; Eurydice is killed by a hidden snake, which is linked to the lust of Aristaeus.

Insight

The snake also symbolizes the knowledge of life and death, perpetuated by sex. Eurydice's death, therefore, is another type of the biblical Fall.

There are variants of the Orpheus myth across the world. Most include the one injunction that the hero cannot resist breaking, which itself is a variant of the mythical theme of the 'one forbidden thing', such as the forbidden room in the Bluebeard story, or, once again, the forbidden fruit recommended to Eve by the serpent. In a strikingly similar version from the Zuni Indian tribe (who almost certainly never had contact with the Greeks), the young brave follows his bride to the land of the dead, and is told not to touch her until they are back in their village. Within sight of the village, she goes to sleep. The young man cannot resist touching her, at which point she returns to the land of the dead for ever.

Insight

Humanity's insistence on doing what is forbidden, often found in myth, could represent rebellion against patriarchal authority, or against the superego. Rather than being a failing, it could represent an essential aspect of humanity – our demand for knowledge.

THE LONELY DESCENT

Underworld descents are usually made alone. The Zuni brave must follow his wife at a distance, and Orpheus does not take any of his old *Argos* shipmates with him. Apart from the obvious fact that we die alone, this represents the 'dark night of the soul', into which one must descend and emerge alone. Orpheus is an artist, and many artists report finding their greatest inspiration after such a descent into the netherworld of the unconscious. The solitary nature of Orpheus' quest is underlined if one thinks of other heroes, so often helped by gods – for example Perseus, who in his conquest of Medusa is assisted by Athene and Hermes. Typically, too, the hero is provided with animal helpers, or with magical implements. Perseus gets his sword, cap of invisibility, bag and shield (see Chapter 5); Theseus has Ariadne's ball of thread (see Chapter 6). Even the Zuni husband is helped by animals – a squirrel and owls.

Orpheus, however, has no assistance. His love for Eurydice is an entirely personal thing. His only magical implement is his lyre, although this is appropriate in that the instrument was invented by Hermes, who as messenger of the gods was able to pass freely in and out of Hades, and as a 'psychopomp' conducted souls there. Other than this, Orpheus has only his voice and his talent. When Inanna descends into Ereshkigal's kingdom, she has to remove all her finery as she goes, so Orpheus' lack of magical implements is fitting: one leaves the human world empty-handed.

THE BACKWARD GLANCE

Different versions of this myth give varying accounts of how Eurydice dies, how Orpheus dies, and even of the outcome of his descent. A few end happily, but most include the key moment of his looking back and thus losing her. This could represent lack of faith, as in the case of the biblical story of Lot's wife, who is turned into a pillar of salt when she looks back. Joseph Campbell sees the Orpheus myth optimistically, as suggesting '... that in spite of the failure recorded, a possibility exists of a return of the lover with his lost love from beyond the terrible threshold.' Indeed, in another Greek version Orpheus is successful, as is the hero of a Polynesian version. Another view is that Orpheus' backward glance is inevitable, since he is human, and since ultimately death cannot be defeated.

ORPHEUS' OWN DEATH

Orpheus dies torn apart by female worshippers of Dionysus. In some versions they are maddened by his constant mourning, and in others they resent his refusal to be comforted by one of them. Their worship of Dionysus is a wild and orgiastic assertion of life, whereas Orpheus' by his insistence on unabated mourning is refusing to move on, denying life. Apollodorus says that Dionysus caused Orpheus's death because Orpheus did not honour him as highly as the sun, while Pausanias mentions Dionysus striking Orpheus dead with a thunderbolt for revealing the Dionysian Mysteries. Ovid lays the blame on the women, but says that Dionysus punished them by turning them into oak trees.

Orpheus' lamenting (or singing) head is like the oracular head of Bran in Celtic myth. It is even more like the head of Mimir – 'He who thinks' – a water spirit who guards a fountain of knowledge in Norse myth. After Mimir dies, Odin preserves the head so that he can still consult it. The image of Orpheus' lamenting head washed towards the sea suggests that, having descended into Hades once, he cannot now die properly. Yet the image is also one of moving towards the source of things, and towards the loss of the individual self in the infinite.

THE ORPHIC MYSTERIES

Orpheus is identified as a mystic as well as a divinely inspired musician. Hence he made sure the Argonauts stopped off to observe the Mysteries on Samothrace, and after his death Mysteries were set up in his honour. The fact that he went to Hades and returned again, albeit without Eurydice, marked him out as possessing knowledge of the next world. Moreover, the continued singing of his severed head after his death connected him with the idea of immortality. His dismemberment connects him to other gods, such as the Egyptian Osiris.

Orphics believed that humans were composed of two elements, the material and the divine. The material element came from their mortal birth and ancestry from the Titans, and the spiritual from partaking in the nature of the divine child, represented by Dionysus, who in one myth was dismembered and eaten by the Titans. Aesthetic and spiritual practices were also encouraged. As in the myth of Er (see Introduction), Orphics believed in a limited form of reincarnation or transmigration of souls from one existence to another, but their ultimate aim was to attain both divinity and immortality.

KEEP IN MIND...

1 Orpheus was the son of Apollo and known for his sweet singing and lyre-playing. On the expedition of the Argonauts he soothed the waves and protected the crew from the Sirens.

2 Orpheus married Eurydice, who was nonetheless pursued by Aristaeus. In her flight she received a fatal bite from a viper, and so she descended into Hades as a shade.

3 The despairing Orpheus resolved to visit Hades to sue for the return of his wife. He did so and succeeded in persuading Hades to release Eurydice, but was told that he must not look at her until they were both back in the outer world.

4 Near the surface, Orpheus could not resist turning to look back at Eurydice, whereupon she was forced to return to Hades for ever.

5 Orpheus was eventually torn to pieces by women in a Dionysiac frenzy who threw his head and harp into the river Hebrus.

6 This is one of many myths involving a descent into an Underworld. These are about confronting death, but also reflect the daily death and rebirth of the sun, and the descent into winter, from which emerges new life in spring.

7 The snake is linked to the lust of Aristaeus, also symbolizing knowledge of life and death, perpetuated by sex, as in the biblical Fall.

8 Such myths frequently involve humans finding it impossible to resist the one thing that they are forbidden to do. On one level this represents the inevitability of death.

9 The women worshipping Dionysus stand for life, whereas Orpheus by his perpetual mourning is denying life.

10 The river into which Orpheus' head is thrown could represent our passage towards the loss of individuality in the ocean of the infinite.

10

In search of the Golden Fleece

The story of Jason is most famously told in the epic *Argonautica* by Apollonius of Rhodes. The earliest account is found in Pindar's Fourth Pythian Ode. It is also recounted in Apollodorus.

Colchis, on the Black Sea, was home to a priceless treasure. It was hidden in a grove sacred to Ares, and nailed to a great oak tree, which some say was the Tree of Life itself. Guarded by a sleep-defying dragon and by the ancient magic of the grove, it was thought to be safe. Yet its whereabouts was known throughout all Greece and beyond, and if any hero succeeded in stealing it, he knew his name would be famous for ever.

Perhaps this had always been Jason's dream. He had been separated from his parents at birth because his uncle had usurped his father's throne, and his parents, pretending that he was stillborn, had smuggled him out to Mount Pelion. There he was raised in secret by the centaur Cheiron, who also instructed him in all the skills and arts of a young hero. When Jason reached manhood, he decided to set out for his homeland, confront the treacherous King Pelias and reclaim his father's kingdom.

On his journey he came to the river Anaurus, which was in flood, and beside it he saw an old woman waiting. Many passed her by, but Jason offered to carry her across. She climbed onto his shoulders and he waded into the water. He was only halfway across when he realized she was very heavy. Soon it was all he could do to keep upright. He lost a sandal struggling out with her on the opposite bank and let her down at last with relief, before going on his way.

Unknowingly, he had just carried the great goddess Hera herself across the water and had already earned her regard and devotion.

Nor was she the only one to take notice of him. When the young would-be hero arrived at the city of Iolchus, heads turned. Although so young, he was already an awesome sight. He stood taller than most men, was armed with two spears, and wore a close-fitting tunic that revealed his well-made limbs. Over this was draped a tawny leopard-skin while, cascading down his back, was his mane of golden hair. Women and children flocked behind him as he made his way to the court of King Pelias.

When he arrived, Jason strode into the palace with all the fearlessness of youth, and confronted his treacherous uncle. Pelias ran his eyes down the boy and felt a rush of fear when he saw he had only one sandal, for he had long ago been warned by an oracle to beware a stranger arriving in this guise. Quickly the wily monarch devised a plan to deal with Jason. Pretending friendship, he asked for his advice on how to get rid of an enemy, to which Jason replied that he would send him in quest of the Golden Fleece. Immediately Pelias decided to send his intrepid nephew on the quest himself. Telling him that the kingdom was troubled by the ghost of Phrixus, who had never received proper burial, he charged Jason with the task of bringing back both the Golden Fleece and the soul of Phrixus with it. He explained that the task was in the interests of the kingdom because afterwards it would become more prosperous and fit for a ruler such as Jason himself. Excited by the challenge, Jason sent to consult the oracle and, on hearing that his quest was propitious, immediately began making plans for the great expedition.

The origin of the Golden Fleece was itself a strange story. The fleece had once belonged to an extraordinary talking and flying ram who had rescued the young prince Phrixus just as he was about to be sacrificed by his father. His horrified mother had appealed to Hermes, who sent the ram in the nick of time, and both Phrixus and his sister Helle climbed on his back and escaped. The children held on bravely as the ram carried them over land and sea but, sadly, Helle lost her grip and fell off into the water at a place which ever after was called the Hellespont. Phrixus, however, kept his seat and landed safely in Colchis. Here he sacrificed the ram to Zeus, who placed it among the stars to become the constellation of Aries. At the same time he gave its fleece to King Aeëtes, who nailed it to the great oak in the sacred grove.

Feeling his quest was justified by the oracle, Jason sent out requests for help over the whole of Greece and beyond, even to the dwellings of the gods themselves. The thought of bringing home such a trophy had wide appeal and Jason soon assembled an outstanding crew composed of the greatest heroes of the day and the sons of the gods. Among them were seers, astrologers and navigators, four sons of the great sea god Poseidon – one of whom, Taenarus, could run across the sea on top of the waves; a son of Apollo, a son of Hermes and another of Dionysus; Idmon, the seer; Periclymenus, who could shape-shift in battle; Zetes and Calais – the purple-winged sons of Boreas, the North Wind; the Dioscuri – Castor and Polydeuces; one woman – Atalanta, a virgin huntress; and Caeneus the Lapith (who had once been a woman), not to mention the supreme poet Orpheus and the greatest hero of the time, Heracles himself. In total, some fifty crew were assembled including, ironically, Acastus, King Pelias' son, who insisted on being one of the number.

Jason then commissioned Argus, the best boat-builder in the land, to construct a large craft which Jason named the *Argo* after its maker, who also came on the voyage. The superb craft was built under the direction of the goddess Athene, and when it was nearly complete, the goddess herself laid a prophetic or 'talking' beam on the prow which had come from the sacred oak of Zeus at the shrine of Dodona.

The day of departure arrived and all the inhabitants of Iolchus turned out to see the Argonauts set out. The crowds parted in awe as the fifty armoured heroes strode past like a moving fire in the sunlight, led by the lion-maned Jason. Never before or since had such a collection of wondrous beings been seen on earth. Women cried and raised their hands to the gods and seers muttered their prophecies as the giant-sized heroes and demigods processed past, carrying their weapons and accoutrements. At their rear strode Argus, builder of the great vessel, a black bull-hide draped over his armour. When they reached the shore, Iphias, the old priestess of Artemis, seized Jason's right hand and kissed it in blessing.

After much feasting and toasting each other with undiluted wine, the heroes raised a pile of stones to Apollo, threw barley upon it and sacrificed two bulls to the god. As the black smoke rose from the burning carcasses, Idmon the seer cried out that it was the will of the gods that they should bring back the Golden Fleece to Iolchus, but that many great trials awaited them. He prophesied that some of them would perish and that he, himself, would never see his homeland again.

Next day they dug a trench for the *Argo*, first positioning polished rollers in place. Some of the crew went into the ship and, reversing their oars, used them as levers to heave the vessel into the trench. Once it began to roll, it rushed like a bird into the sea, but the other heroes held it back with strong ropes until they had all boarded. Then they raised the mast, unfurled the sail and were carried off, the sail bellying in the wind.

The oarsmen set the sea churning like a seething cauldron, while their metalled arms dipped and rose like bright flames in the sunlight. They made good speed for many days and nights, but before entering the ocean proper they stopped and set up an altar to Poseidon, asking him to speed their journey.

After this they travelled on for many weeks until they reached the island of Lemnos, where they decided to go ashore. Lemnos at that time was populated entirely by women – they had killed all their men after discovering their unfaithfulness with some Thracian slave women. At first, the islanders were wary of the Argonauts, thinking they might be angry Thracians come to punish them for the slaughter but, realizing they were not enemies, the women welcomed the crew ashore. The heroes set themselves athletic games and trials and generally demonstrated their prowess. After this the women invited them to their beds. Their purpose was to repopulate the island, and its queen, Hypsipyle, chose Jason as her consort. The heroes spent many months on the island, long enough for Hypsipyle to bear two sons. Indeed, they might have remained there permanently had not Heracles, who had spent most of his time guarding the *Argo*, stormed angrily onto the island and reminded them of their quest.

Their next port of call was Samothrace, where, encouraged by Orpheus, they were initiated into the Mysteries. After this they passed through the Hellespont under cover of darkness. Arriving at a rocky peninsula, they went ashore and were welcomed by King Cyzicus and invited to join his marriage feast. Just as they were enjoying the food, wine and entertainment, a tribe of fearful six-handed giants launched a sudden attack, whereupon the Argonauts immediately sprang up and fought with them, killing them all. After receiving the king's undying gratitude they departed, but made such poor headway that Tiphys, the chief navigator, decided to turn about and make for the peninsula again. Landing on an unknown shore in darkness, they were mistaken for pirates and engaged in battle. However, when dawn broke, they were horrified to discover they had mistakenly killed their former host, King Cyzicus. They held a great funeral for him which lasted three days, and cut off their hair in lamentation. But his grief-stricken bride, Cleite, hanged herself, at which it was said the nymphs of the island wept so copiously that they created a fountain with their tears, which was named after her.

The Argonauts continued sadly on their voyage, making propitiation to the goddess Rhea for the deaths of the six-armed giants which had led to this further slaughter. Then, to restore their warrior resolve, they undertook a rowing contest which was so arduous that all the heroes gradually dropped out until only Jason and Heracles were left. But just as Jason began to tire, Heracles broke his oar and they were forced to beach the *Argo* at Cios while he went ashore to find wood for a new one. His close companion Hylas disembarked with him and went to fetch water, after which he disappeared. Heracles, who greatly loved the boy, stayed so long on the island calling and searching for him that in the end the Argonauts decided to leave without him. But Heracles' search was in vain, for the beautiful young Hylas was never found, having been pulled down into a spring by a nymph who had fallen in love with him.

The Argonauts' next encounter was with the Behryces, a warlike people who lived on the Bosphorus and whose king, Amycus, challenged all comers to a boxing match. Polydeuces took up the challenge and managed to overcome and kill him, after which the Argonauts battled successfully with the Bebryces and celebrated their victory.

The Argonauts then sailed on up the Bosphorus until they came to Salmydessus, where they were invited by the half-starved, blind prophet Phineus to dine with him. But as soon as they sat down to eat, two huge winged creatures, hag-faced and with women's breasts hanging between their wing feathers, swooped down on them and seized their food. They then made off leaving a vile stench behind them. These were the Harpies, vengeful winged creatures, half-woman and half-bird. At once the two sons of Boreas flew up into the air and, calling on their father's powers, blew the Harpies away across the sea. They chased and harried them as far as the Strophades, making sure they would never return. In gratitude for his deliverance, Phineus gave the Argonauts invaluable advice for the rest of their journey across the Bosphorus to Colchis, beginning with how to negotiate the fearful wandering rocks known as the Symplegades.

The Symplegades were also called the Clashing Rocks, because they would rush together and crush any ship that tried to sail between them. As the Argonauts drew near, the fearful rocks loomed into view through thick clouds of white spray. When the Symplegades roared together, dark caverns gaped opened beneath them and the sea surged inside, boiled up, and surged out again. The *Argo* began to be tossed towards the rocks, but the heroes held the ship back with their oars while Euphemus, the far-sighted, climbed the prow and, waiting until the rocks began to draw apart again, released a young dove. The bird flew straight as an arrow between the two cliff faces so that when they clashed together they caught only the tip of its tail. As soon as the rocks began to open again the heroes began rowing for their lives. Orpheus, leaning forward at the prow, summoned music with shaking fingers to slow the rocks down while the *Argo* raced through at high speed. Halfway through the ship foundered but an arc of water leaped up beneath it, shooting it forward so that the clashing rocks only sheared off the tail end of its stern.

After this the Argonauts sailed on to the land of King Lycos. Here they were made welcome and were able to replenish their stocks. But the place proved fateful, for Idmon, Apollo's son, wandered off and was killed by a wild boar. Here, too, Typhus the helmsman fell sick and died. The Argonauts held great funeral rites for the men, piling stone mounds over their bodies, sacrificing sheep and planting the wild olive tree as a token. Wearied and despairing, some of the heroes lost heart at this point, but the others urged them on, reminding them that they had been warned of these perils.

After this the crew survived many more adventures. They passed the land of the Amazon women, where they were removed from danger by the thrust of the tide. They also passed a cave entrance into Hades from which an icy wind issued. They passed other lands such as Sinope, named after the virgin who had cleverly outwitted Zeus, and that of the Tibareni where the men suffered the pains of childbirth instead of the women. At times, it seemed they were magically carried away from peril, while at others they seemed to be deliberately delivered into it. Some adventures required the special talents of individual heroes, while others required their combined powers.

One day, as they were rowing on calm water, they heard a whirr of metal and Oileus cried out, dropping his oar and clutching his left shoulder as a pointed shaft entered it. They looked up and saw a great brass-feathered bird clattering its huge wings above them. Immediately the heroes aimed a dozen arrows in its direction, but they bounced off it. Angered, the bird let out a hideous scream and hailed more sharp-pointed feathers at them. Then other birds appeared flying noisily towards them. Seeing that attack was useless, the heroes covered themselves with their shields, interlocking them to form an impenetrable roof. Protected in this way, they rowed on and put to shore on the island of Ares, as Phineus had instructed them.

They beached the *Argo* safely, and slept the night on the island undisturbed. The next day a great storm arose and four young men were cast ashore, half-dead after a shipwreck. The Argonauts revived them and discovered they were the four sons of the long-dead Phrixus and that their mother was Chalciope, daughter of King Aeëtes, who owned the Golden Fleece. Jason invited them to join his expedition and, in gratitude for their rescue, they agreed, although fearing that this would greatly anger their grandfather.

Before long the Caucasian Mountains came in sight and they saw the god Prometheus tied to them and heard his screams as he endured his punishment for stealing fire for humanity.

Having crossed the Black Sea, the Argonauts finally reached Colchis. Feeling as if they had arrived at the end of the world, they moored in a concealed place and held counsel regarding the final stage of the quest.

Commentary

The legend of the Argonauts is as old as the *Odyssey*, in which it is, in fact, mentioned. Like the *Odyssey*, the *Argonautica* is a hotchpotch

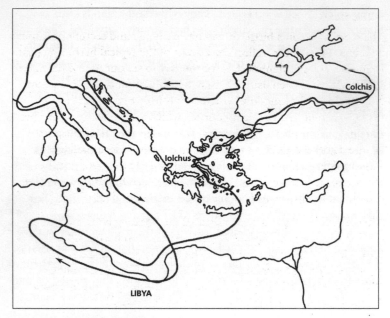

Figure 10.1 Possible route taken by the Argo

of accumulated myth and folk tale. It is also a type of otherworldly journey, or *immrama*. But, unlike the Celtic mystical journeys which only take the hero to a symbolic Otherworld, its route is also a geographical one. As such, it reflects the early explorations of Minoan and Mycenaean seamen. Although the outward journey is easily mapped, different versions have arisen of the return journey, influenced by the colonization and exploration of the seventh and sixth centuries BCE. Pindar, in his Fourth Pythian Ode, says the Argonauts were a semi-mythical people known as the Minyans.

Insight

The voyage of the Argonauts is thought to be a historical one and to have taken place in the thirteenth century BCE. The ship set off from Iolchus, now Volos, in Thessaly, where a Mycenaean Bronze Age settlement has since been discovered.

THE HERO

The story of Jason's birth, threatened early life and secret upbringing by a wise older tutor, reflect the advent of the typical hero. The next step, on reaching manhood, is for the boy to set out to find his father. If his father has been usurped, then his obligation is to avenge him and take over the kingdom which is rightfully his. As part of this, the hero is required to take a journey which symbolically marks his transition from youth to maturity. During the course of the journey he undergoes tests of prowess, ingenuity and wisdom, and learns valuable spiritual and psychological lessons. The type of goal at the end of the journey may vary, but the successful attainment of it usually yields the rewards of marriage and a kingdom.

After fulfilling all the requirements of the budding hero, including seeking to avenge his father, Jason is sent out on his quest by the trickery of his usurper uncle. The hero is often pushed into his journey of discovery by an enemy, either through a taunt or challenge. Here, King Pelias is evidently colluding in Jason's own dream of glory, which is why Jason is so enthusiastic.

SUPERNATURAL AID

The supernatural aspect of the journey is clear from the beginning. Before setting out, Jason is careful to invoke the aid of the gods. He consults the oracle to see if his journey will be propitious, after which he sends invitations to gods as well as men to accompany him. Most importantly, the *Argo* is constructed in part as a magical boat with the help of Athene. Before the Argonauts set out, all the proper rituals are observed, and the *Argo* is finally launched on a propitious day after appropriate sacrifices have been offered. The influence of the two goddesses Hera and Athene is particularly strong throughout the voyage, but there is a good balance between the male and female deities involved since Zeus' oracular beam has been incorporated into the ship.

Insight

Athene acts as personal guardian to Jason and the Argonauts. She completes the building of the *Argo* by adding the all-important 'talking prow' which comes from her father Zeus' sacred grove of oak trees at Dodona.

Figure 10.2 The Argo

THE ROLE OF HERACLES

Between them, the company boasts a dazzling array of skills and talents. Together, the Argonauts denote the varied qualities and strengths needed by the individual hero. For example, the sons of Boreas represent agility, Idmon, mystical understanding, and Orpheus, spiritual and creative powers, while Heracles represents physical strength. Some versions of the story say that at the beginning there was contention as to whether Jason or Heracles should be the leader, but that Heracles graciously gave way to Jason. The question of leadership was a vital one, for the success of the voyage, as with the successful integration of the individual personality, relies on a harmonious balance of attributes. Thus, when Heracles declines leadership he is acknowledging that sheer physical strength must take its place alongside qualities such as wisdom and intuition.

However, in terms of the quest, Heracles' role is a vital one. It is significant that he alone declines to 'marry' the women on the island of Lemnos, and guards the boat instead. He is the one, therefore, who can call the heroes back to the quest when they are in danger of being waylaid by women. Heracles reminds them that they are pledged to the journey and that the women are 'strangers'. (Unknown to the heroes, the women are also murderesses.) The role of woman in terms of the journey is very important, for she can act either as the ultimate goal or as a snare for the hero. It is therefore vital that he can distinguish between the two. In this respect, Queen Hypsipyle signifies the temptation of settling down prematurely to a life of marital and sexual comfort, instead of fulfilling the quest. A similar temptation is offered to the Celtic hero Maeldun and his companions on their journey to the Otherworld, when an island queen prevents their departure by throwing a sticky ball for Maeldun to catch and then winding the boat back into shore.

After Heracles has made the heroes leave Lemnos, Orpheus suggests they go to Samothrace and partake in the Mysteries. Although the island is out of their way, they agree to go. This episode shows that the Argonauts were careful to maintain a balance between the physical and spiritual aspects of their journey. But later, having inadvertently killed King Cyzicus, they fall into despair. To combat this, they decide on a rowing contest. Jason is overly competitive in this and annoys Heracles by trying to prove he is equally strong. It is just after this that the Argonauts decide to abandon the great hero, thinking they can manage without him. This is a foolish decision because it amounts to a rejection of physical prowess. Ironically, immediately afterwards they are subjected to a test of strength by King Amycus and, although Polydeuces manages to defeat him, his victory is hard won. The heroes discover the full consequence of their rejection of Heracles only after they reach Colchis.

THE HARPIES

Appropriately it is Zetes and Calais, the two sons of Boreas, who have to deal with the Harpies – for it was they who persuaded the Argonauts to leave Heracles behind. Here the Harpies represent the negative aspect of the female, which preys on the blind Phineus, denying him sustenance. They are actually punishing Phineus for his treatment of his wife because, on the instructions of his mistress, he has imprisoned her and blinded their two sons. In early mythology the harpies were the winged deities of the storm winds. Here they demonstrate the vindictiveness of the vengeful female and provide a warning of the fate that awaits Jason.

THE UNCONSCIOUS

The sea is the great symbol of the unconscious, and any voyage taken on it can be seen as a psychological journey. The Argonauts have to use a range of skills in order to meet the strange trials that face them. In the case of the brass birds, they have to use their ingenuity, while, with the Symplegades, they need both wit and magic. Orpheus' music has the power to delay the rocks while Athena later tells them it was she who caused the arc of water which propelled them to safety. After their successful passage between them, the rocks were said to have stopped wandering and become rooted.

Insight

The heroes' adventures become less naturalistic and more fantastical as they progress. When they begin to encounter the harpies and the brass birds, this is an indication that they are moving deeper into the territory of the unconscious.

THE RAM AS SACRIFICE

The earlier story of Phrixus, as the king's son, being prepared for sacrifice is not an unusual one in mythology. The ritual of human sacrifice was common in very early times and was connected with fertility and the round of the seasons. Annually the king, or a surrogate, was sacrificed in winter or early spring, to represent the death of the year. A new king would replace him, thus ensuring the renewed fertility of the earth, symbolized by the Great Goddess or Earth Mother. In Greece and elsewhere the ritual involved the victim wearing a ram's fleece. The ritual took place at the spring equinox, the time when the constellation Aries was astrologically prominent. Later, a ram was substituted for the human victim. This changeover is reflected in the well-known biblical story of Abraham, who was allowed to sacrifice a ram instead of his son Isaac.

KEEP IN MIND...

1 In this myth Jason, the king's son, has been smuggled out of the kingdom by his parents who are seeking to save him from Pelias, his usurping uncle. He is brought up by the centaur Cheiron, who tutors him.

2 When Jason is old enough he sets out to reclaim his father's throne but is instead sent off by the wily Pelias in quest of the Golden Fleece.

3 Jason takes on this quest and invites a distinguished company composed of heroes and sons of gods to accompany him.

4 The company sail in the *Argos*, a magical ship which bears the oracular 'talking prow', a gift from Athene taken from the sacred grove of her father Zeus at Dodona.

5 The Argonauts undergo numerous adventures on their outward journey, and endure many hardships. Finally they cross the Black Sea and arrive at Colchis, home of the Golden Fleece.

6 Although the journey is a geographical one and therefore possibly part historical, it is also a type of mystical journey, or *immrama*, a journey of self-discovery.

7 Jason, as the hero, is on a journey which symbolically marks his transition from youth to maturity. On the way, he undergoes tests of prowess and wisdom.

8 Collectively, the Argonauts represent the varied qualities needed by the individual hero. Losing Heracles is tantamount to losing physical strength.

9 Because the sea is the symbol of the unconscious, the voyage of the Argonauts can be seen as a psychological journey. The strange nature of some of their adventures suggests this.

10 In ancient Greece, an annual ritual took place to mark the spring equinox – the time when the constellation Aries (the Ram) was astrologically prominent. It involved the victim wearing a ram's fleece. In later times, a ram was substituted for a human victim.

Jason and Medea

The Argonauts, having arrived in Colchis, discuss how to obtain the object of their quest.

After consultation the Argonauts decided to approach King Aeëtes directly and request that he give them the Golden Fleece. Jason therefore promptly set out for the palace, taking with him two of the Argonauts.

They made their way inland guided by the sons of Phrixus. As they strode towards the city of Aea, Hera caused a mist to come up which hid them from view. Before long they found themselves at Circe's plain, which was a strange and eerie place. Through the mist they could see the outlines of willows and osiers with dark shapes hanging on their upper branches. As they drew nearer, they saw that they were shrouded corpses. The entire plain was hung with them. Some had had their bones picked clean by the vultures, some were decayed beyond all recognition, while some were still dripping blood. The sons of Phrixus told them that it was the custom in that land only to bury women and to expose male corpses to the air.

As they came to the end of the plain the mist cleared and they could see Aeëtes' palace ahead of them on top of the sacred hill of Helios. Built by Hephaestus in honour of the sun god, it was fronted by a series of courtyards with rows of tall columns stretching away on either side, while above them brass triglyphs supported the great stone roof. Ascending a series of marble steps, the men entered a courtyard with four fountains in it. The fountains had these properties: one sprayed white milk into the air, another ran with wine, the third ran with scented oil, while the fourth one gave out warm water by day and cavern-cold torrents by night. Passing through the courtyard, the party strode boldly into the palace, where they found King Aeëtes seated on a silk-covered couch, surrounded by servants.

At first Aeëtes was amazed to see his grandsons returned from their voyage so soon. But after they had told him of their rescue, he invited Jason and his two companions to feast with him. During the meal, he complained about an enemy tribe who were refusing to give him tribute. At this point one of Phrixus' sons spoke for the Argonauts, telling his grandfather of their mission and saying that the warriors would help him subdue his enemy if he would grant them the object of their quest, the Golden Fleece. Aeetes turned on him in fury, and immediately ordered the Argonauts off his land on pain of having their hands cut off and their tongues ripped out. At this, Jason and his companions sprang to their feet, weapons raised.

But suddenly there was a commotion from the inner hall and in swept Medea, priestess of the goddess Hecate. Taller than her father the king, with hair falling like a black cloak down her shoulders and her dark skin tattooed with the marks of the goddess, she approached the great table.

'There is a better way,' she said. 'Command this man to yoke the brass-footed bulls of Hephaestus and plough the Field of Ares with them even while they breathe fire upon him. Tell him that afterwards he must sow the field with dragon's teeth and then conquer the army of warriors that springs up from them. Tell him, if he can do all this, he may then approach the sacred grove.' Her eyes flashed in the torchlight and an answering smile crossed Aeëtes' face.

'Very well,' he said. 'It seems I was over-hasty. My daughter is right. If you can prove yourself able to accomplish these things, the fleece is yours for the taking.'

Then, seeing he had no other way open to him, Jason lowered his spear and bowed his head.

'If those are your terms,' he said, 'I accept.'

He looked up, and his eyes met those of Medea.

That night the sorceress left the palace and, wrapping her cloak around her, made her way to the ancient grove of Hecate. There, flaming with passion, she called on her own and the deeper arts of the goddess and made a potion for Jason from the double-stalked saffron crocus. This Caucasian flower had first sprung from the drops of blood falling from Prometheus on the mountainside. She mixed the juice and put it in a phial. Then she stole back to the palace, where her sister Chalciope met her and offered to help her.

Meanwhile, Jason returned to the *Argo*, accompanied by Argus, the son of Aeëtes. They took counsel with the Argonauts and all agreed that the task was beyond Jason's powers. Argus urged him to seek help from Medea and the heroes agreed with this. Only Idas felt it was unmanly to ask help of a woman instead of calling on the strength of the god Ares, and argued passionately against the plan. But at that moment a dove fell from the sky into Jason's lap and the hawk that was pursuing it fell too, becoming impaled on the stern. Mopsus the seer declared that this was a sign from the gods that Jason should seek help from the sorceress. Although Idas again berated them, saying, 'Do you look to doves and hawks to save yourselves from contests?', the other Argonauts agreed that Jason should go to Medea.

Meanwhile, Chalciope had discovered that Medea was already planning to help Jason. So she sent word to Jason that Medea would meet him at dawn at the Temple of Hecate. Jason went and found Medea standing in the early light, half-veiled, like a goddess.

'You must go to the river at dusk and bathe yourself,' she said. 'After that you must dig a circular pit and slay a young ewe in it, offering it to Hecate and pouring out a libation of honey. Then you must leave, and should you hear Hecate approach accompanied by the baying of all the hounds of Hades, you must on no account turn round.'

Then, holding out a phial to Jason, she continued:

'At dawn you must cover yourself with this ointment. You must also anoint your spear, your shield and your sword with it. It will protect you from the might of the fire-breathing oxen for one day, but for one day only. When you have yoked the beasts and ploughed the Field of Ares with them, you must sow the dragon's teeth that my father will give you. As soon as you have done that an army will spring up from the earth, armed and raring for battle. But you must throw a great stone quoit into the middle of them so that they turn on each other. When most of them have been killed, you can go in and kill the rest. This is the only way you can outwit my father and achieve the tasks he has set you.'

'My thanks to you, lady,' said Jason. 'For this, I will make you honoured above all women. Your name shall be famous throughout my land, when I return home in triumph.'

'And am I only to enjoy a remote honour?' said Medea drily. 'Am I to be abandoned here, when I expect faithfulness? Am I to be cast aside, when I expect the rites of love?'

Then Jason realized that there was a high price to pay for the help she offered. He looked on her and a thrill of fear went through him, for she was dangerous as well as beautiful, and he was awed by her. Then, taking her hand, he swore by all the gods of Olympus that he would never desert her, saying, 'It shall be as you desire. I will take you back to my homeland, where we will have our marriage feast in great splendour. After that you will sit beside me in honour and help me rule Iolchus.'

So it was that, armed with her instructions, Jason subdued the fire-breathing brazen-footed bulls of Aeëtes, ploughed the great field, and sowed the dragon's teeth. When the earth-born soldiers sprang up, he threw a great boulder in the middle of them and, after they had turned on each other, he rushed in and single-handedly finished the slaughter. All the citizens of Aea were amazed at his prowess and a great cheer went up as he returned in triumph to King Aeëtes. But the king, still fearing that the Argonauts were after his kingdom, determined not to keep his word but to send his soldiers out that night to burn the *Argo* and slay the heroes.

When Medea discovered this, she went secretly to the Argonauts and told them of her father's plan. She urged them to seize their treasure straight away. Then she guided them to the Grove of Ares, where they found the Golden Fleece guarded by the fierce, unsleeping dragon. They drew back at this, but Medea approached the serpent, singing incantatory music to charm and quiet its great hissing. Then she took some fresh juniper leaves and squeezed out drops of juice on the monster's eyelids, so that it finally went to sleep. After that, Jason sprang into the grove and took the fleece from the sacred oak, escaping with it to the *Argo*, whereupon the Argonauts began rowing away from Colchis as fast as they could, taking Medea with them.

It was not long before Aeëtes discovered the loss of both the Golden Fleece and his daughter. He set out in pursuit, but sent a party of men ahead led by his youngest son, Apsyrtus, who caught up with them at the mouth of the Danube. Medea received him aboard the *Argo* and, aided by Jason, she killed and dismembered him, scattering his body parts in the ocean. The pursuing Aeëtes stopped to gather up his son's remains, and the *Argo* escaped.

But the terrible crime of fratricide had been committed and a pall fell upon the heroes. As the *Argo* sailed on, the voice of Zeus issued from her speaking prow, commanding them to go to the enchantress Circe, to be purged of the murder, or else they would be harried by endless tempests and prevented from returning home.

Circe lived on the island of Aeaea, where she practised her arts and created strange primitive beasts out of primeval slime. Her palace was made of polished black stone which shone in the moonlight. Inside, its walls were stained with the blood of ritual offerings. When the Argonauts arrived on the island, they went to the palace and found the great sorceress in the inner sanctuary, dousing burning herbs with sacrificial blood. When they told her Zeus had commanded them to come for purification, she reluctantly fetched a young sow and severed its head. She sprinkled its blood on the heroes' hands and then made propitiatory offerings and burned atonement cakes. Praying for protection against the wrath of the Furies, she called on Zeus the Cleanser and invoked his protection for the heroes. But when she had finished the purification and discovered whom it was they had murdered, she sent them away from her in horror.

The Argonauts resumed their journey and came at length to the lonely, enchanted island of the Sirens. As they drew near, they could hear the women singing their irresistible melodies. But Orpheus snatched up his lyre and began weaving his own powerful music to drown out their songs. In this way the Argonauts sailed past in safety. Only Butes, son of Teleon, was unable to resist jumping overboard and swimming towards the terrible creatures, but at the last moment he was snatched out of danger by Aphrodite and taken to the island of Sicily.

Again they sailed on, successfully avoiding the twin perils of Scylla, the multi-headed monster, and Charybdis, the fatal whirlpool, but soon after this the Colchian fleet caught up with them on the island of Scheria. At first, Alcinous, the king of the island, welcomed the Argonauts, but then the Colchians put their case to him and asked him to help them capture Medea. While the king was debating the situation, he confided in his wife Arete that, if Medea was still a virgin, he would feel honour-bound to return her but, if not, he would let her stay with Jason. Arete stole out of her chamber and told this to the Argonauts, whereupon the heroes prepared a hasty wedding ceremony in a sacred cave, and Jason and Medea, who had planned to celebrate their nuptials in Iolchus, were obliged to consummate their union that night.

After this the Colchians gave up pursuing them and they went safely on their way until a freak wind blew them off course and onto the Libyan desert. They landed so far inland that they became completely stranded. This was too much for the heroes who, having struggled so gloriously for so long, finally gave up in despair and lay down, preparing for death. But Jason had a visionary dream in which he was visited by three nymphs, who called themselves the guardians of Libya. They told him to take heart and to instruct the Argonauts to recompense their mother who had borne them for so long in her womb. When Jason awoke, he called the heroes together and told them his dream.

'But', he said, 'they disappeared before I could find out who our mother is.'

'Surely our mother is the *Argo*, who has borne us across the sea in her womb!' cried the heroes.

Then, although their strength was weakened, they devised a plan which was to roll the *Argo* overland until they could put her to sea again. The powerful Argonauts propelled the great ship for twelve days and nights across the desert, until they reached a salt lake. Here, so exhausted and parched that they were unable to continue, they called on the nymphs of the place to give them water. They were answered by the Hesperides, who had until recently guarded their golden apples along with the giant serpent Ladon. They told the heroes that Heracles had killed Ladon and robbed them of their treasure, but had opened up a spring nearby. This precious water saved the heroes, who afterwards tried vainly to find Heracles until they were helped to relaunch the *Argo* by the fish-tailed sea god Triton who pulled it across the desert and into the Mediterranean Sea.

Back on the water and with their homeland almost within sight, the heroes' next threat came from the brass-armoured giant Talos who patrolled the borders of Crete, throwing rocks at any vessels who dared to sail near. But Medea contrived by her arts to kill him, summoning the death spirits who caused him to pierce his ankle on a rock, after which his life-force drained out of him.

The weary but triumphant Argonauts finally reached home after this, only to find there was no one to greet them. Learning from a boatman that Jason's parents had both been killed by King Pelias, Medea told them to keep their homecoming secret and offered to avenge Jason's parents herself, by means of sorcery.

The Argonauts having agreed, she turned herself into an old crone and, accompanied by twelve maidens that Queen Arete had given her, processed into the city just before nightfall carrying a wooden image of Artemis. Once inside the walls, the women began raging around the city like the Furies, causing such terrible uproar that Pelias, roused from sleep, demanded in fear what the meaning of this was. Medea told him that Artemis had come to rejuvenate him. She demonstrated this by cutting up an old ram and boiling it in a cauldron, from which, miraculously, a young lamb emerged. Medea then sent the king to sleep by means of a drugged potion and commanded his three daughters to cut him up into pieces. Two of them consented and, after they had done the deed, she told them to go in procession up to the roof of the palace, bearing torches, and make invocations to the moon while the cauldron boiled. Innocently, they obeyed her, but the torchlight was a signal to the Argonauts, who on sight of it immediately rushed in and took the city.

After that, instead of taking his place as ruler of the kingdom, Jason gave it to Pelias' son Acastus. Then, because Acastus threatened to avenge his father's death, Jason fled to Corinth. There he lived in state with Medea for ten years until the day came when he broke his solemn oath to the gods and betrayed her. But that is another story.

Figure 11.1 Medea prepares to rejuvenate the ram

Commentary

From the moment the Argonauts arrive at Colchis, it is evident that they are lacking in the heroic principle. Deciding against the use of either force or cunning, they naively plan to ask King Aeëtes outright for the Fleece. This seems to be prompted by an over-reliance on the sons of Phrixus, who not only lead them to the palace, but make the request on Jason's behalf. The heroes would not have behaved like this if Heracles had been with them, for Heracles not only represented the male principle of force but also the conscious power of discrimination. He would have opposed Jason's reliance on Medea on both grounds.

CADMUS

In his fear of performing the final feat, Jason contrasts strongly with the hero Cadmus, who had gone before him. Cadmus had previously gone to Boeotia and killed the Dragon of Ares that guarded a spring. At Athene's bidding, he had then sown half the dragon's teeth in the earth, after which armed men sprang up who turned on each other when Cadmus threw stones among them. The remaining dragons' teeth were given by Athene to Aeëtes who made them part of Jason's trial. Cadmus performed his task single-handed and without help. Afterwards he had to serve Ares for eight years as appeasement for killing his dragon, but eventually he was rewarded with the kingdom of Thebes and the hand of Harmonia, daughter of Ares and Aphrodite.

In his success, Cadmus demonstrates the ideal path of the hero. For the journey of the hero was understood as being taken on both an outer and inner level. Outwardly, he developed his strength and bravery by wresting material treasure from a dragon or other threatening enemy. Inwardly, having developed his male consciousness, he was supposed to use it to overcome the negative feminine, represented by the dragon, in order to rescue the fair inner feminine, which represented his soul.

Lacking Heracles, who would have provided not only physical strength, but also the discrimination to reject Medea, Jason finds he is cornered into a position where he feels unable to carry out the tasks imposed on him. Medea has manoeuvred him into this, knowing that he will need her help to complete them. When the Argonauts debate whether he should rely on her, only Idas seems aware of the humiliation. The heroes have moved so far away from their heroic ideals that they are content to rely on the powers of a woman. Medea, however, is no ordinary woman.

MEDEA

Medea's power and her hold over Jason prevent her from being seen as the typical female reward for the hero who has proved himself. In her dealings with Jason, Medea seems to be acting not out of love but out of possessiveness. Instead of helping him as, for example, Ariadne helps Theseus by giving him the thread to bring him back out of the labyrinth, Medea takes over. First, she anoints him so that he cannot be harmed. Then, when he has carried out the required tasks, she enchants the dragon for him.

The fact that something in the relationship is wrong is borne out by the heroes' opinion of her. The Argonauts are wary of her and unhappy about taking her with them. Their unease is justified when she commits the outrageous crime of dismembering her half-brother. By not punishing her for this, however, they effectively collude in the act and have to suffer the consequences. Zeus, angered by the crime, ceases to help them, so their journey home becomes extraordinarily protracted. Her act is, however, a macabre version of what Joseph Campbell terms the 'obstacle flight' of the hero, in which he throws items behind him in order to delay his pursuer – or, symbolically, to delay a confrontation with divinity for which he is not yet ready.

THE ROUTE HOME

Because they are being pursued, the Argonauts are unable to return through the tight pass of the Bosphorus so, according to Apollonius, they return across Europe via the river Danube, which he believed connected the Black Sea to the Adriatic. Both ancient and modern scholars have debated this route. Taking the geography of the journey literally, cases have been made for the course across Europe, somehow hauling the *Argo* from river to river, then coming down in the Adriatic, or even the far side of Italy, and looping into the Libyan desert before returning across the Mediterranean. Another claim involved a truly epic journey in which the *Argo* headed north across Russia, emerging via the river Volga into the North Sea and rounding Scandinavia and the British Isles before returning past the coast of Spain. Recently, an even more extraordinary theory has been advanced, suggesting that the Argonauts went west, rather than east, to a place called Colchis in South America.

Insight

Whether the route can be convincingly charted geographically or not, the legend records the fact that the return journey was made unnecessarily difficult by the presence of Medea and that the Argonauts were taken off course until they received purification from Circe.

CIRCE

Circe was King Aeëtes' sister and Medea's aunt. She was also said to be the daughter of Helios, the sun god. Her island was located by the ancients off the west coast of Italy (now Monte Circeo on the mainland). Most famously, she received Odysseus and turned his men into pigs. Outwitted by Odysseus, she became his lover for a year. She was obviously beautiful and dangerous, like her niece. In this story, she appears in her professional capacity, acting under orders from Zeus. She was said to have performed regenerative rites in which the initiate was dowsed with bull's blood. Her gruesome cemetery at Colchis is said to be dedicated to Hecate (see below).

FURTHER PERILS OF THE JOURNEY

After being purified, the Argonauts, like Odysseus after them, have to brave the island of the Sirens and then the twin perils of Scylla and Charybdis. The island of the Sirens was also located off the west coast of Italy. These fatal and fascinating creatures were related to the harpies, being bird-women. They were far more alluring, however, having the power to enchant with their singing. Although irresistible, there is a tale that they competed musically with the Muses and lost, whereupon the Muses made crowns for themselves with some of their golden feathers. In this story they also lose to Orpheus, whose music overpowers theirs.

The multi-headed Scylla was originally a beautiful nymph, turned by Circe, for reasons of jealousy, into a monster with six heads. Charybdis was a whirlpool that sucked the seawater down three times daily and was the more fearful because it threatened the entire ship.

Insight

Ovid says the Sirens were originally companions of Persephone who were given wings by the gods to search for her after she disappeared. But others say their wings were given to the Sirens as a punishment for having colluded in Persephone's abduction.

Having successfully negotiated these hazards, the heroes head back towards Greece and meet the remnant of Aeëtes' fleet waiting for them on the island of Scheria (now Corfu). Its king, Alcinous, then becomes an arbiter between the two sides. It is clear that Aeëtes is pursuing the Argonauts to avenge Apsyrtus and to reclaim his daughter, not to rescue the Golden Fleece. In order to keep hold of Medea, the Argonauts arrange a furtive wedding in a sacred cave. Such a secretive wedding seems appropriate to the Dark Mother aspect of Medea (see below) and is another indication of the strange nature of her union with Jason.

The next adventure, in which the Argonauts become stranded on the Libyan desert, is extraordinary. It appears that the feminine principle, symbolized by the sea, has failed them. It is notable that Medea is unable to help at this point and that, instead, the fair triple goddess of the land instructs them to honour their mother, meaning the *Argo*. This is an interesting connection, especially because the dragon guarding the Golden Fleece is described as being the same length as the *Argo*. Symbolically, therefore, the two can be considered counterparts of each other. Also, unlike Medea, the goddess of Libya helps them by directing them back towards their masculine powers, for the feat of rolling the ship across the desert for 12 days requires all their strength. This renewal of their masculine energies links them with Heracles, who they discover has arrived just before them, killed the serpent Ladon and seized the treasure of the golden apples. Heracles' feat demonstrates what is expected of a hero in such circumstances and can be seen as an ironic comment on Jason's failure in this respect. Nevertheless, after this the Argonauts resume their reliance on Medea.

THE CAULDRON OF REGENERATION

Medea's use of the cauldron for the dismemberment of Pelias links her to the ancient stories of the cauldron of regeneration, which was traditionally a feminine symbol. It featured particularly strongly in Celtic myth and was connected with the god Bran and the witch goddess Ceridwen. It was also the prototype of the Holy Grail. Its regenerative powers were those of the ancient triple-aspected goddess of life and death who ritually received the offering of the dismembered male in token of the regeneration of the seasons and the refertilizing of the earth. It is this aspect of the goddess that Medea demonstrates in her dismemberment of both Apsyrtus and Pelias. (For the ritual sacrifice of kings, see Chapter 10.)

THE DARK MOTHER

The role of the Dark Mother or Goddess pervades this story. In psychological terms, it reflects a masculine, patriarchal fear of the feminine which results in the splitting of the original goddess of life and death into two distinct aspects – fair and dark. Here, she is represented in her dark form only. Worse than that, she is made into a triplicate of dark forms because the heroes have to contend with the three most powerful sorceress figures in Greek mythology: Circe, Medea and Hecate. As priestess of Hecate, Medea represents the fearful negative feminine which lurks in the deepest recesses of the unconscious. It is this primitive and possessive side of the Great Mother that can trap the emerging male psyche and arrest its development. Medea has power over the serpent because she is allied with it. When Jason fails to kill it, he is held prisoner by the negative anima which she represents. Because he does not really win the Golden Fleece by his own strength, his success is a partial one.

HECATE

The Dark Mother aspect is also seen in the figure of Hecate. Hecate was originally a benign triple goddess, associated with the moon and with Artemis. She was also the friend of Demeter and helped her find Persephone (see Chapter 8). She then became Persephone's attendant, after which she became inextricably connected with the Underworld. By the fifth century BCE she was identified as the goddess of ghosts and shades, being linked with the dark rather than the bright moon. She was still represented in triplicate, but was placed at crossroads so that she faced in three directions. She became associated with the ghostly night hunt, in which she was accompanied by the red-eyed, baying hounds of hell. In the story of Jason, she is seen in this dark aspect, being associated with death, sorcery and witchcraft. (In this capacity, she directs the three witches in Shakespeare's *Macbeth*.)

Circe's grove or cemetery is said by Robert Graves to be dedicated to Hecate, who may have been her mother. It is certainly full of willows, which are associated with her, and also with death. Jason has to traverse this fearsome grove before he reaches Aeëtes' palace, the grove is a ghoulish demonstration of the female association with death. The corpses were wrapped in untanned ox-hides and left in the tops of the willows, to the element of air. Because this

Colchian practice was confined to male corpses, it shows a sharp division between the sexes and their connection with the elements. The element of earth has long been considered a female element, and that of air, masculine. It is because of this Colchian practice that the Greeks, who favoured burial for both sexes, believed the soul of Phrixus was still wandering, having been denied burial.

Insight

The practice of leaving corpses to the air still holds today in many cultures. For example, the Jains deposit their corpses in high towers, relying on vultures to devour them, and the Lakota Indians similarly used to leave their corpses to the air.

THE GOLDEN FLEECE

The Golden Fleece originally belonged to the magic talking ram that was sent by Hermes to rescue Phrixus, who was about be sacrificed. The ram is a strong symbol of masculine energies and attributes. It is linked with Ares, the god of war (see Chapter 1). The name of Ares was given to nearly every place in or near Colchis, and the Golden Fleece was hung in the Grove of Ares. The attributes of the god Ares are also found in the astrological sign of Aries – represented by the ram. The constellation of Aries represents the masculine qualities of strength, leadership, competitiveness, spontaneity and initiative.

THE HERO'S JOURNEY

Because the ram is identified with the male principle, Phrixus' journey represents that of the hero, for he is transported to Colchis by means of masculine energy. (It is possible his sister Helle fell off the ram because the journey was not hers to take.) Once in Colchis, Phrixus marries the king's daughter and becomes heir to the kingdom, thus fulfilling his hero's journey. Jason's own hero's journey is flawed because the masculine energy symbolized by the Fleece seems to have become the goal or treasure itself rather than the means of achieving a goal. The hero's treasure was usually connected with the feminine.

Insight

Recent research has discovered that, in early times, fleeces were used by the Colchians to trap gold dust swirling along the river bed. Accordingly, it is possible that Jason and the Argonauts may have been on a quest for the gold rather than the Fleece itself.

THE END OF THE STORY

As a flawed hero, Jason reaches the ends of his quest in only partial triumph. After he returns home, he finds his parents dead and relies on Medea to kill the usurping king. He is then prevented from ruling his own kingdom because he is forced to flee the vengeance of Acastus, Pelias' son. Taking refuge in Corinth he eventually falls in love with the king's daughter Creusa (or Glauce) and decides, too late, to put Medea aside in order to remarry. Here, belatedly, Jason seems to be attempting to shift into the normal process in which the hero returns in triumph, reclaims his kingdom and marries a king's daughter. But his attempt to find his true inner feminine comes too late, for he cannot escape the negative anima. Medea retaliates by giving his bride a poisoned dress that sets her on fire and burns the palace with the king in it. After this she is said to have killed her own children out of vengeance. But an alternative version says that, before fleeing Corinth, Medea entrusted her children to a process meant to ensure their immortality, but that, after she had gone, the Corinthians killed them. When this crime became known, it made the Corinthians so unpopular that they bribed Euripides to rewrite the story, putting the guilt on Medea.

DEATH OF JASON

Unlike other heroes, Jason has an ignoble ending. Years later, weary and defeated, he sits on the shore beneath the old *Argo*, now beached and rotting, remembering with sadness the Argonauts' former glories. The oak prow, that once delivered Zeus' oracular instructions, falls from the ship and kills him.

KEEP IN MIND...

1 The second part of the myth tells how the heroes, having arrived in Colchis, have to cross the fearful Grove of Circe with its hanging corpses, before reaching the palace of King Aeëtes.

2 King Aeëtes is at first reluctant to grant them the Golden Fleece in return for delivering them from an enemy, but Medea, the king's daughter and priestess of Hecate, persuades her father to help them.

3 She instructs Jason and aids him with her magic so that he can carry out a series of tasks: subduing the fiery bulls, ploughing and sowing the Field of Ares with dragon's teeth and finally, when an army of soldiers subsequently springs up, making them fight each other and then single-handedly finishing the slaughter.

4 In return for Medea's help, Jason agrees to marry her. However, this is against King Aeëtes' wishes so the Argonauts seize the Golden Fleece and abduct Medea.

5 Aeëtes pursues the Argonauts on their way home but, to slow him down and help them escape, Medea kills and dismembers her brother. The crime of fratricide turns the gods against the Argonauts so they seek cleansing from the sorceress Circe.

6 After enduring many more adventures, including having to carry the *Argo* overland, the Argonauts eventually reach home where Medea helps them kill the usurping King Pelias. Jason gives the throne to Pelias' son, Acastus. However, because Acastus threatens to avenge his father's death, Jason flees to Corinth where he lives in state with Medea for ten years.

7 By relying too much on the dark and magical powers of a woman who is also a sorceress, Jason shows himself as a flawed hero.

8 By colluding in Medea's crime of fratricide, the Argonauts have to bear the consequences. Zeus ceases to help them and their journey home becomes hugely difficult and protracted.

9 Medea is a type of the Dark Mother or negative anima. Together with Circe and Hecate she is one of a trio of dark feminine forces which eventually overwhelm the heroic aspects of the warriors.

10 Because aspects of this myth can be charted geographically, it may be based on an actual historic journey in search of gold.

The Judgement of Paris

This famous and intriguing story which is claimed to be the cause of the great Trojan War is found in Apollodorus and is also mentioned by Pausanias.

When the dark beauty Hecuba, the wife of King Priam, was pregnant, she had a terrifying dream. She dreamed she gave birth to a firebrand and awoke screaming that the city of Troy was burning to the ground. Alarmed by this, her husband consulted his son, the seer Aesacus, who told him the baby would one day cause the destruction of his country. Accordingly, Priam ordered that the child should be put to death. So, after the boy was born, he was given to the chief herdsman, Agelaus, to be killed. Agelaus left the child on Mount Ida to die from exposure but, returning five days later, found the boy still alive and took him home, where he brought him up secretly. As a young man, Paris became noted for his extreme beauty, wit and prowess.

At about this time the wedding of Peleus and Thetis, the hero and the sea goddess, was celebrated on Mount Pelion. All the gods and goddesses were invited with the noted exception of Eris, the goddess of strife, who was hideous and disagreeable. Angered at being left out of the nuptials she strode into the middle of the wedding feast and threw a golden apple into the assembled company. It landed between the three most powerful goddesses, Hera, Athene and Aphrodite. Picking it up, Zeus found it was inscribed 'For the Fairest'. Wisely deciding not to judge between the three deities himself, Zeus nominated the beautiful Paris as arbiter, but first he sent Hermes to enquire whether he would be willing to act as judge. Paris agreed and so a time was set for the three goddesses to appear to him on Mount Ida.

When the day came, Paris sat himself on a boulder and waited with beating heart for the arrival of the three great deities. All at once a great light appeared which covered the entire mountain. At first Paris was blinded, but then the goddesses cloaked their light in cloud so that he was able to look at them.

First Hera, the great queen, approached him and flaunted her beauty in front of him. Radiant with glory she made him a promise. If he awarded her the apple, she would grant him wealth and power. He would rule over the greatest kingdom on earth. Paris felt the excitement of this and his ambition rose up and yearned for her gift.

After that, grey-eyed Athene approached him, drawing near and bending down, so that he might look into the magical depths of her eyes. She promised him victory in all battles, together with glory and wisdom – the three most precious gifts a man could have. This time Paris felt his mind leap with desire for the riches of knowledge and the glory of prowess.

Then it was the turn of Aphrodite. Hanging back a little, she tilted her head so that her hair fell forward, concealing a blush on her face. Then she loosened the girdle of her robe and beneath it, Paris caught sight of her perfectly formed breast, white as alabaster.

'Paris,' she said, and her voice seemed to sing inside his head. 'Give me the apple and in return I will give you the gift of love. You will possess the most beautiful woman in the land, a woman equal to me in perfection of form. With her you will experience the greatest delights of love-making. Choose me, Paris, and she will be yours.'

Then Paris, overpowered by the intoxication of her words and her beauty, found himself handing her the apple without even pausing to reflect on his decision, guided only by the strength of his desire.

So it was that Paris awarded the Apple of Discord to Aphrodite, and Hera and Athene became his implacable enemies. True to her promise, Aphrodite gave him Helen, the most beautiful woman living on the earth at that time – but, in order to enjoy her, he had to snatch her from her powerful husband, Menelaus.

So began the terrible ten years' war between the Trojans and the Greeks in which many a brave hero lost his life, including Paris himself, and after which the great hero Odysseus wandered the seas for a further ten long years before returning home.

Commentary

This brief episode, which is to have such far-reaching consequences, begins on a suitably ominous note. Hecuba's dream is reminiscent of other prophetic dreams and portents. As is usually the case, those involved take drastic steps to prevent the awful prophecy coming true. This is the case with the Celtic Deirdre, whose beauty causes similar strife, and Oedipus (see Chapter 4), who as an infant is exposed at birth in a similar way to Paris. Like Oedipus, and other heroes, Paris grows up unaware of his true parentage. Ironically, he is even said to have unwittingly attended his own funeral games, finally held by his real parents for their 'long-dead' son! As in other cases, too, the gods ensure that mortals are unable to avoid their fate.

Insight

Attempting to challenge and outwit the power of the gods by defying a prophecy or oracle (as did Oedipus) was seen as an act of hubris. In Greek tragedies the haughtiness and vanity of those who show irreverence to the gods inevitably result in their humiliation and downfall.

GODDESSES DISHONOURED

The full extent to which humans are ruled by the gods only becomes clear when we learn that Aphrodite set up the contest, presumably knowing that she held the trump card. She did so in order to punish Tyndareus, husband of Leda, for dishonouring her. Pausanias relates that Tyndareus put fetters on Aphrodite's statue in her temple because he felt that her amorous powers should be confined to marriage. The outraged goddess decided to make all three of his daughters unfaithful to their husbands. The most famous daughter was Helen of Troy, although strictly speaking her father was probably Zeus, who seduced Leda in the form of a swan on a night when she also slept with her husband.

The marriage at which the fateful apple is produced is unusual, being between a mortal man and a goddess. The failure to invite Eris, Strife (echoed in the fairy tale of Sleeping Beauty), represents a dishonouring comparable with Tyndareus' treatment of Aphrodite. The implication is that even destructive deities are essential to the psyche and to society, and will make their presence felt if denied.

Similarly, strife is a necessary part of marriage. Eris is associated with Ares, god of war, who in turn is amorously connected to Aphrodite.

THE BEAUTY CONTEST

The contest which Eris initiates sets the three goddesses against each other. In myth, goddesses frequently appear in threes, representing aspects of a single deity. Thus, although Hera, Athene and Aphrodite represent quite different forces, the competition may reflect a time when they were less divided. Paris has a difficult choice. Hera, wife of Zeus, is the goddess of marriage and the home, and as such is always smarting from her husband's sexual adventures. Athene is a virgin goddess of war and wisdom. Aphrodite is the goddess of sexual love, also associated with physical beauty in all its forms. Yet her affairs with the war god Ares, and her engineering of the Trojan War (as well as lesser conflicts), suggest the close relationship between sexual love and conflict.

The apple thrown by Eris is perhaps related to Eve's apple, representing a Fall from unity to disunity. The contest itself resembles other mythical contests, especially that between three Celtic heroes, including Cúchulainn, concerning which of them is the greatest hero. Here the role played by Eris in the Greek myth is paralleled by that of the mischief-maker Bricriu.

Insight

Because Aphrodite is behind the whole thing, it seems that the contest is unequal from the start. Contrary to the story's title – 'The Judgement of Paris' – Paris is so overpowered by Aphrodite that he is unable to exercise his judgement. We could see this as a metaphor for 'falling in love'.

In another version of the story, Aphrodite cheats by revealing herself naked except for her magic girdle. In an even more intriguing version, found in Euripides and Apollodorus, Hera, angry with Paris for choosing Aphrodite, creates a phantom Helen, whom he weds, while the real Helen is spirited away to Egypt by Hermes on the orders of Zeus. This implies that Paris does not relate to the real woman, but to a phantasm of his own imagination. In Jungian terms, she is the projection of his anima.

KEEP IN MIND...

1 The myth concerns King Priam's son Paris who, it was prophesied, would bring about the destruction of Troy. He was cast out as a baby and brought up secretly by a herdsman.

2 At the wedding of Peleus and Thetis, Eris, the goddess of strife, angry at not having been invited, threw down the apple of discord among the three chief goddesses, Hera, Athene and Aphrodite.

3 Zeus invited Paris to choose which of the three was the fairest and deserved the apple. He chose Aphrodite because she offered to give him the most beautiful woman in the world to be his lover.

4 Paris fell in love with Helen, wife of Menelaus. Their subsequent elopement gave rise to the Trojan War.

5 Aphrodite set up this contest to punish Helen's father, Tyndareus, who had put fetters on her statue, intending to limit her power of love to married couples.

6 Tyndareus was married to Leda, who had been seduced by Zeus in the shape of a swan. Thus, ironically, Helen was probably Zeus' daughter, not Tyndareus'.

7 The story, as with so many other myths, shows that the fate decreed by the gods cannot be changed. To try and outwit them is tantamount to hubris.

8 In myth, goddesses frequently appear in threes, representing aspects of a single deity. Hera, Athene and Aphrodite may at one time have been less divided.

9 The apple thrown by Eris causes a fall from unity to disunity, and may therefore be related to Eve's apple in Genesis.

10 In another version of the myth, Hera creates a phantom Helen with whom Paris falls in love, suggesting he is infatuated not with a real woman but with a phantasm, a projection of his own anima.

13

Ares and Aphrodite

Aphrodite was the most beautiful, most voluptuous and most alluring of all the goddesses, which is not surprising as she was the goddess of love. Yet she was married to a god who was far from being her equal in looks – the lame and misshapen Hephaestus. The son of mighty Zeus and his wife Hera, Hephaestus was nonetheless born crippled, so that Hera, ashamed of her offspring, hurled him from the heights of Olympus into the sea, where he was cared for by the nymphs Thetis and Eurynome. Here he honed to a fine art the natural talent for all kinds of metalwork that was to make him the blacksmith of the gods. For nine years he invented marvellous devices for the two nymphs, and at the same time planned his revenge on his mother, Hera.

One day Hephaestus sent his mother a gift of a golden throne. She received it with wonder and sat in it immediately, only to find that she was stuck fast. Only her son could release her, and he refused to leave his ocean home. Ares tried to drag him up by force, but Hephaestus saw him off with burning brands lit from the fire in his smithy. Dionysus had more success, plying the lame god with wine so that he became drunk and could be brought back to Olympus on a mule. Even then, he stubbornly refused to free Hera until promised a bride who would go some way to compensate for his lameness and ill treatment – the most beautiful of goddesses, Aphrodite.

Now, while limping Hephaestus, with his massive, overdeveloped torso and his puny legs, was seen as a figure of fun among the gods, Ares was acknowledged to be well made and handsome. As the god of war and strife, he was not especially popular with the other gods, but his good looks had their appeal, at least for Aphrodite. Perhaps Ares still bore a grudge against Hephaestus for getting the better of him, or perhaps he was just irresistibly drawn to the soft and silky delights of Aphrodite – such a far cry from the harshness of the battlefield. Whichever is the case, he began to woo her with gifts, and before long, clearly preferring the handsome warrior god to her ill-favoured husband, she succumbed.

Unfortunately for the amorous couple, very little escapes the eye of Helios the sun god. He quickly reported their affair to Hephaestus, who limped furiously off to his forge to brood his revenge. Stoking the fire with his hurt and anger, he set about fashioning a net of chains so fine that they could not be seen, yet so strong that not even a mighty god could escape their hold. He suspended the invisible net above the marital bed – the bed in which he expected the guilty pair to renew their embraces as soon as his back was turned – then sought out Aphrodite.

'Dear wife,' he told her, 'I am going to visit my beloved Lemnos, whose people hold me in high regard. I will be gone for some time.' Saying this, he pretended to make his departure.

Ares saw Hephaestus leave, and was quick to seize the opportunity. He found Aphrodite sitting alone, took her in his arms, and led her to the great bed; he had no trouble in finding his way there. There, the god and goddess enjoyed each other at length, until finally they fell asleep exhausted. But while they slept so peacefully, the net of Hephaestus closed silently around them, holding them in its inescapable grasp.

They were awoken by the angry voice of Hephaestus. Alerted by his spy, Helios the sun god, he had hurried back, having first summoned other gods with the promise of an entertaining sight.

'Father Zeus,' he announced, 'and all you other immortal gods, come and see for yourselves the ridiculous and shameful sight that I will reveal to you. Great Zeus' daughter Aphrodite dishonours me, her lawful husband, because I am lame and lack the good looks of her lovers. Only my parents are to blame for that! Yet faithless Aphrodite prefers Ares because he is handsome and well made. Come and see the happy couple drowsy with love! Oh, yes, they love to lie in each other's arms, but I do not think they will do so for any longer than they have to now. Yet there will they lie until Zeus returns the dowry I paid for his baggage of a daughter.'

The assembled gods – and only the gods, because the goddesses had stayed away for shame – gazed on the naked and humiliated lovers and burst into an uproar of laughter.

'See how Hephaestus, despite his lameness, has trapped the fleet-footed Ares. How the mighty are fallen!' they said, one to another. Taking up the joke, Apollo questioned Hermes: 'Messenger god, giver of great gifts, would you not happily lie in such chains in order to enjoy the love of sweet Aphrodite?'

'Indeed, Lord Apollo,' replied Hermes, 'if only I had the chance, I would happily lie in chains three times as strong, and all you gods could come and watch!'

This started up the gods' laughter again, and it was only quietened when sombre Poseidon eventually told the master smith to free his prisoners, promising that Ares would be made to pay him damages.

'Do not ask me to do this,' pleaded the reluctant Hephaestus. 'He will break his promise, and I will have no remedy once he is free.'

Only when Poseidon promised to stand surety for Ares was Hephaestus persuaded to release the shamefaced lovers. With his powerful arms he plucked off the net, and immediately the pair sprung away in different directions. Ares angrily fled to the land of the warlike Thracians, while Aphrodite took refuge in her temple at Paphos, in Cyprus, where she was bathed and anointed by the three Graces, and dressed once more in the rich garments that befit a goddess.

Commentary

The liaison between Ares and Aphrodite is a clear case of opposites attracting. Their opposed natures have traditionally been shown in astrology, where they relate to the planets Mars and Venus, by the symbols used for those planets: the cross of matter above the circle of spirit for Mars, and the reverse for Venus.

Insight

The symbols for Mars and Venus have long been used to represent male and female, though in the Mars symbol the cross has now become a tilted arrow.

THE GODDESS OF LOVE

Aphrodite is the goddess of sexual love, also connected more widely to the psychic drive towards union and harmony. Though married to Hephaestus, she bore him no children and had many affairs. Her principal lover was Ares, to whom she bore Harmonia, Phobos and Deimos, but she was also said to have borne children to Dionysus, Hermes and Poseidon. More famously, she became besotted with the beautiful young huntsman Adonis, in one version even while he was a baby. It seems it was not in her nature to be faithful, her drive being always to form an erotic union with any male to whom she was attracted, regardless of the consequences. Commenting on her affair with Ares, Michael Vannoy Adams, writes in Lucy Huskinson (ed.), *Dreaming the Myth Onwards: New Directions in Jungian Therapy and Thought*:

> *The Aphrodite variety of love is not the 'moral' love of fidelity in marriage. That is the Hera variety of love. The numerous infidelities of Zeus offend the Hera variety of love. From that perspective, the Aphrodite variety of love is amoral, even 'immoral'. In one aspect, Aphrodite is the goddess of affairs*.

Adams goes on to comment that when Jung said to Freud, 'The prerequisite for a good marriage … is the licence to be unfaithful,' he was trying 'to reconcile the Hera variety of love with the Aphrodite variety of love'.

Aphrodite was also known to encourage this erotic love in others, both mortal and immortal (hence the word 'aphrodisiac'), and even to inflict it on them. On Mount Olympus only the virgin goddesses Athena, Artemis and Hestia were immune to her powers. All the other gods were at various times made to fall helplessly in love as a result of her influence.

While on the whole the ancient Greeks saw love as a benign, desirable and even necessary phenomenon, there is an element of ambivalence in its portrayal in myths. Hence Zeus' decision to make Aphrodite fall in love with the Trojan prince Anchises, so that Aphrodite would know the torment of desire for a mortal. Aphrodite seduced him in the form of a mortal and bore him a son, the hero Aeneas. This ambivalence is also seen in the story of Aphrodite's liaison with Ares. There is a sweetness in surrendering the ego, but at the same time this involves a loss of autonomy, and even of reason. This loss is symbolized by the net, as invisible as love is inexplicable, yet immensely powerful. This ambivalence about love is also seen in the great amusement of the gods at the sight of the trapped lovers. Love, while all-consuming to those in love, or in lust, can seem a little ridiculous to onlookers – a fact playfully acknowledged and exploited by Shakespeare in such comedies as *Twelfth Night* and *A Midsummer Night's Dream*.

Another aspect of sexual love is jealousy. This is represented in the myths of Aphrodite by her insistence on being honoured by mortals. So, for example, she caused the women of Lemnos – so beloved of Hephaestus – to have a foul body odour because they had failed to worship her. She punished Myrrha for neglecting to honour her by making the young woman fall in love with her own father, Cinyras. When the Propoetides (daughters of Propoetus) ignored her worship, she turned them into the first prostitutes (see Chapter 13). She was also jealous of rivals: she punished Eos, goddess of dawn, for sleeping with Ares by making her subject to repeated infatuations with mortal men.

Insight

Aphrodite's well-known jealousy no doubt inclines the gods to be less than sympathetic when she is trapped in the net of Hephaestus.

THE GOD OF WAR

While Aphrodite was a goddess of love, Ares was a god of war. But whereas the virgin goddess Athene symbolizes the disciplined and reasonable use of force in defence, Ares embodies the bloodlust, frenzy and chaos of battle. His Roman equivalent, Mars, received far more respect from the Romans than Ares did from the Greeks – which tells us a lot about the priorities of the two cultures. His own father, Zeus, tells him in Homer's *Iliad*, 'To me you are the most objectionable of all the Olympian gods, for you love strife, war and battle. You have the obstinate and unmanageable temperament of your mother Hera.' Despite being the god of war, Ares does not even enjoy much success in battle. In the *Iliad* he is flattened by a blow from a huge stone cast by Athene, and in an account by Hesiod he is wounded in the thigh by Heracles and has to be helped into his chariot and driven back to Olympus.

The union of Ares and Aphrodite could be seen as a way of tempering their extremes. Psychologically, the urge towards union is balanced by the ego's need to assert itself. In a Jungian sense, if Aphrodite is all anima, Ares is all animus; together they form a whole. In another sense, too, this union of opposites is inevitable. Love can often lead to strife, and less often strife to love. In myth, we see this in the Judgement of Paris (see Chapter 12), whereby Aphrodite brings about the beginning of the Trojan War. We also see this in literature and drama, for example in *Romeo and Juliet*, in which love and hate seem inextricable.

HEPHAESTUS AND POSEIDON

The role of Hephaestus in this story is also of interest. Although he invites the gods to witness the shame of Ares and Aphrodite, he is also to some extent an object of mockery himself, since he has been cuckolded because Aphrodite spurns him in favour of the more attractive Ares. However, despite often occasioning the laughter of the gods, he is essential to them as a forger of weaponry. Nor is he an ordinary blacksmith. As his invisible net shows, he combines practical skill with inventive ingenuity. Symbolically, this combination overcomes the blind passion of love. Without this element in the human psyche there would be no advances in technology.

Insight

On a cosmic level Hephaestus could represent the forces that fuse the raw material of the universe into galaxies.

Finally we come to Poseidon. As the sea god – named Neptune in the Roman pantheon – he could be seen as having a special connection with Aphrodite. Although Homer names her as the daughter of Zeus and the Titan goddess Dione, a more interesting story in Hesiod holds that, when Cronus castrated Uranus and cast his father's severed genitals into the sea, Aphrodite sprang fully formed out of the resulting foam (see Chapter 2). He is seen in myth as a stern and powerful god. Perhaps the fact that he has the last word in this episode reflects the role of the sea as a symbol of the unconscious. On the other hand, his main concern is to free Ares, rather than Aphrodite, so it may be that the aggression that Ares represents is linked to Poseidon's role as the bringer of violence in the form of storms and earthquakes.

Insight

In modern astrology, Neptune is to some extent seen as a higher form of Venus, representing spiritual, as opposed to sexual, love.

KEEP IN MIND...

1 Ares is the son of Zeus and Hera, and is the god of war and battle, symbolizing the assertive ego.

2 Aphrodite is either the daughter of Zeus and Dione, or was born from the severed genitalia of Uranus.

3 Aphrodite is the goddess of sexual love and symbolizes the urge towards union.

4 The Greek Ares and Aphrodite are equivalent to the Roman Mars and Venus, though the Romans had more respect for Mars than the Greeks had for Ares.

5 Hephaestus is the son of Zeus and Hera, a lame smith god, respected by the gods for his craftsmanship but ridiculed for his lameness.

6 Ares and Aphrodite are tricked by Hephaestus and trapped in his invisible chain net, to be humiliated before the gods.

7 As opposite forces, Ares and Aphrodite are irresistibly drawn to each other. The negative aspect of their passion is represented by the imprisoning net of Hephaestus.

8 Hephaestus represents creative ingenuity on the physical plane.

9 Once freed, the couple speed away in different directions, symbolizing psychic separation.

10 Poseidon is an authority figure who is particularly concerned to free Ares.

14

Pygmalion and Galatea

The best-known version of this myth is found in Ovid's *Metamorphoses*.

Cyprus being the birthplace of the beautiful goddess of love, Aphrodite became known as the Lady of Cyprus. Her temple was forever adorned with offerings. Myrtle trees, doves, sparrows, horses and swans were all sacred to her, and it was said that the beauty of the island derived from the beauty of their patron goddess. It was therefore a dreadful insult when the daughters of Propoetus, living in the city of Amathus, refused to worship her. Aphrodite was outraged by this and determined to punish them. She cursed the Propoetides, and turned them from modest maidens into prostitutes – and these were the first prostitutes known to man. Soon the young women became so shameless through their harlotry that they lost all female modesty and were no longer able to blush. As time went by, they became as hard as flint and as heartless as stone, until finally they turned completely into flint stone.

Now an ardent young sculptor named Pygmalion, who also lived on the island of Cyprus, was so appalled by the behaviour of the Propoetides that he resolved never to marry but rather to remain celibate all his days. Instead, he threw his energies into his art. A brilliant artist, his masterpiece was the statue of a woman carved out of pure white ivory. Her skin was translucent, her limbs exquisite, her hair cascaded down her shoulders in a frozen thrill of stone. It was as if he had put all his thwarted desire for women into this work of utter perfection. He called his statue Galatea, and so lifelike was she that she seemed only a step away from a living being. He sometimes imagined that she was secretly alive but, unlike the Propoetides, was so modest that she felt even unable to move. Again and again he found himself touching her, almost expecting the warmth of flesh beneath his hand, only to be met by cold ivory.

Pygmalion became obsessed with his creation. He whispered words of love to her and brought her offerings, the kind of beautiful things that he thought delighted women – pretty shells and polished stones, brightly coloured flowers, lilies, coloured balls and beads of amber. He robed her in fine clothes and decked her with jewels. He put rings on her delicate fingers, a necklace around her swanlike neck, a pendant to hang between her exquisite breasts, and fixed a fine pearl earring to each perfect ear. He laid her gently on a couch covered in purple silk. There he cradled her, calling her his darling, and, caressing her gently, believing that if he pressed too hard, he might bruise her beautiful white skin.

Then the day of Aphrodite's annual festival arrived. Because Aphrodite was the most revered deity on the island, it was a great and important festival. Incense wafted high into the air. All of Cyprus joined the parade, leaping and dancing along the streets, praising their Queen of Love with songs and music. Torches were lit so that the celebrations could continue into the night. In Aphrodite's honour, pure white heifers with their horns specially gilded were driven to the holy altar at her temple where they were slaughtered as an offering to the lovely goddess.

Pygmalion, like the other Cyprians, brought his own special offering to the festival – and his was rich and costly. Having laid it at the temple precinct, kneeling before the altar, he prayed that mighty Aphrodite might deign to hear him. With fear and trepidation, he begged her to grant the longing of his soul and bestow on his ivory love the gift of human life.

As soon as he had dared his prayer, the bright flame burning on her altar flared up and leaped into the sky. Three times the flame soared up and with each thrilling leap increasing hope rose in Pygmalion's heart.

As he left the festival and made his way home, he hardly dared believe his bold request might actually have been granted.

He ran into his house and there his darling was, lying on his couch as he had left her. He hurried over and knelt to kiss her. Was she still cold and hard, or was there a tiny hint of warmth? He caressed her breast. Could it be softer now, or was it just his imagination? Her flesh seemed faintly warm. It felt as though her skin were yielding to his touch, softening like wax in the sun. Fear and hope fought within him. Could it really be true? Could she be coming into life – for him? He stroked her beautiful body, touched her breasts again. And now there could be no doubt that she was slowly warming into life beneath his hands. A pulse began in her, faint at first, then stronger, and now the blood was indeed flowing through her veins and, by degrees, her ivory hardness was transformed completely. The fair and beautiful statue became a living woman in his arms.

Pygmalion fell to his knees in shock and joy, pouring out a paean of praise and gratitude to Aphrodite who had heard his prayer and granted him such a prize.

Then, with tears of happiness flowing from his eyes, he turned again to his love and put his lips to hers. This time he felt response. Kiss for kiss she gave back while a maiden's blush suffused her white cheeks and made her lovelier to him than words could say.

After bringing Galatea to life, Aphrodite laid her blessing on the pair and granted them a child. Nine months after Pygmalion had first held Galatea in his arms and known her love, a baby boy was born. They named him Paphos.

Commentary

APHRODITE

Aphrodite, the goddess of love, was a notoriously jealous goddess. As such, she was quick to wreak vengeance on those who refused her worship. Thus she curses the Propoetides for their neglect of her and turns them into strumpets. Ovid cleverly brings this tale in as a prologue to his story of Pygmalion. The myth of Pygmalion then becomes a reversal of the former tale. Aphrodite, having reduced her non-worshippers to stone, is keen to show her power to bring maidenly modesty out of stone, when supplicated by a devotee.

In this myth, she seems to be presiding over pure, monogamous love, rather than extramarital affairs and intrigues – which can also be attributed to her influence (see Chapter 13). As goddess of love, she naturally rewards and blesses all her devotees overcome by the obsession caused by that powerful emotion. Harlotry, however, which is not driven by love's fervour, she frowns upon. This myth can therefore be seen as showing her reward for devotion to the power of love and the punishment for its misuse.

PAPHOS

The myth of Pygmalion and Galatea is sometimes seen as a founding myth of the city of Paphos. After she rose from the sea, Aphrodite was said to have landed at Paphos, which became the centre of her cult. Her cult was established there before the time of Homer, who mentions it in the *Odyssey*. The city of Paphos was praised by the poets in word and song and became a place of pilgrimage for the whole of the Aegean. Worship at Aphrodite's cult site, which included an oracle, continued at Paphos in an unbroken tradition up until 391 CE when the Romans outlawed all pagan shrines. The remains of her once huge and impressive temple can still be seen there today.

AN EARLIER VERSION OF MYTH

In an earlier version of the myth, attributed to Apollodorus, Pygmalion was king of Cyprus. He became so obsessed with the goddess Aphrodite that he had her statue removed from her temple and placed in his palace. He laid it on his couch and made love to it. The spirit of Aphrodite entered her statue and brought it to life. Two children were born from this union, a son called Paphos and a daughter called Metharme.

THE INSPIRATION OF THE MYTH

The story of Pygmalion and Galatea has inspired artists down the ages. It was the subject of art works by Edward Burne-Jones, Rodin and Goya among others. Not surprisingly – given the theme of bringing life to stone – there have been numerous sculptures depicting the awakening of Galatea. The myth has had a powerful influence in opera and ballet, too, with works such as Delibes' *Coppélia*, which is based on Offenbach's *Tales of Hoffmann*, in which Hoffmann falls in love with a mechanical doll called Olympia.

Besides painters, sculptors and musicians, the myth has also inspired poets and authors down the ages, with works such as Dryden's poem 'Pygmalion and the Statue' – a translation of Ovid; Robert Browning's poem 'My Last Duchess', and novels such as Oscar Wilde's *The Picture of Dorian Gray*. Both Browning and Wilde use portraits rather than statues. Browning's poem is about a woman whose husband has in effect replaced her with a painting so that she can perpetually please and remain under his control. In Wilde's novel, Dorian's portrait takes on a life of its own, making the mortal man the unchanging original.

Insight

The ancient Greeks believed that the artist's function was to attempt to rival creation itself. They believed the power of art was magical and the artist's skill godlike and inspired. Today the myth still raises deep questions, inviting an exploration of the relationship between life and art.

THE WINTER'S TALE

Shakespeare famously took inspiration for *The Winter's Tale* from Ovid's version of the myth. In the play, Leontes' wronged wife, Hermione, disappears and is thought by him to be dead. Sixteen years later she reappears, having been suspended in time, frozen into a statue. She movingly returns to life again, in response to Leontes' love for her and his deep penitence for his former harsh treatment of her. As with Galatea in the original myth, Hermione's restoration to life seems to be linked to her husband's desire for her and comes in response to his awakened regard for her value.

THE VICTORIAN POPULARITY OF THE MYTH

The myth seems to have reached a peak of popularity in Victorian times, particularly with works for the stage. In 1871 W. S. Gilbert wrote his play *Pygmalion and Galatea*, in which Galatea comes to life only to find she causes such disruption in the sculptor's marriage that she decides to turn back into stone. This was subsequently parodied and turned into a burlesque, *Galatea, or*

Pygmalion Reversed, in which the roles of Galatea and Pygmalion are reversed. Galatea creates Pygmalion, who comes to life but is abominably vain and causes havoc among women until returned to his original state.

GEORGE BERNARD SHAW

Perhaps the most famous adaptation of the myth is Shaw's play *Pygmalion*, which he wrote in 1912 and which was later most notably adapted in 1956 into the well-known musical and subsequent film *My Fair Lady* (1964). In the original play, Eliza Doolittle, a cockney flower-seller from Covent Garden, is taken home by Professor Henry Higgins, a phonetics expert, who bets his friend Colonel Pickering that he can train her to speak properly, and pass her off as a duchess in high society. Eliza eventually passes the test but ends up refusing to marry the high and mighty Higgins. The play is intended to highlight the independence of women and is a variant on the original myth.

Shaw was therefore horrified when, in its first production in 1914, the ending of his play was altered to a happy one. Herbert Beerbolm Tree, the play's producer, argued: 'My ending makes money; you ought to be grateful.' To this Shaw replied: 'Your ending is damnable; you ought to be shot.'

In his essay 'What Happened Afterwards', written in protest, Shaw argues vehemently that, if Eliza was worth her salt and had really come to life like Galatea, she would, having achieved autonomy and being faced with a choice between two suitors, marry the young romantic Freddie Eynsford-Hill, rather than Henry Higgins. In his final sentence, Shaw declares: 'Galatea never does quite like Pygmalion: his relation to her is too godlike to be altogether agreeable.'

However, despite Shaw's intentions regarding his work, subsequent productions have all featured the changed ending, rendering them more faithful to the original myth.

More recently, elements of the same story in which education plays a large part in the transformation of a lower-class woman can be seen in Willy Russell's play *Educating Rita*.

PROSTITUTION

Some have found in the myth the theme of 'the prostitute with a heart of gold'. This concerns the idea of the transformation and reforming of a street girl into a lady. Shaw's *Pygmalion* can be seen to have such a theme at its heart and the same theme inspired the 1990 film *Pretty Woman*, in which the heroine's former prostitution is openly acknowledged.

AUTOMATA

The myth of Pygmalion stands behind the horror and fascination inherent in the figure of the mechanical robot. In fact, it could be argued that all films or plays depicting automata spring from this myth. Its influence can be seen in stories such as Mary Shelley's *Frankenstein* and, more subtly, in twentieth-century films such as Hitchcock's *Vertigo*.

As with Shaw's play, it has been used particularly to point up feminist issues. An example of this is the powerful horror film *The Stepford Wives* (1975), in which women in the town of Stepford are turned into automata by a consortium of their husbands. The film is an indictment of the hostility of men towards the new freedom sought by women, its message being that men would prefer their women to be like biddable statues or automata.

Indeed, the original myth would seem to support this view, suggesting that Galatea is completely compliant, having no autonomy, no power over her own life, and is created by Pygmalion solely to please his fantasies. Against this, it could be argued that Pygmalion is a worshipper of Aphrodite and that as such he is the servant of love and of women. It could also be said that Pygmalion's disdain for all women, based on the behaviour of the Propoetides, is transformed when he falls in love with Galatea. This, in turn, provokes in him a proper devotion to Aphrodite and makes him elevate his regard for women in general.

The myth of Pygmalion and Galatea is rich in possible meanings. It adapts itself to each age and, while of particular appeal in the Victorian era, when women were beginning to find their voice and raise themselves to the status enjoyed by men, it is equally suited to the modern era, in which the on-going struggle of women to be treated not as pretty dolls but as equals to men continues.

KEEP IN MIND...

1 The myth concerns the sculptor Pygmalion, who carves the statue of a beautiful woman with whom he subsequently falls in love. He beseeches Aphrodite to bring her to life and his request is granted.

2 In Ovid, this myth is contrasted with Aphrodite's punishment of non-worshippers, the Propoetides, whom she turns first into harlots and then into flint.

3 The cult of Aphrodite was based in the city of Paphos on Cyprus, but her fame went throughout the Aegean.

4 The myth has inspired artists, musicians and sculptors down the ages. It reached a peak in Victorian times, particularly with works for the stage.

5 Bernard Shaw's play *Pygmalion* is based directly on the Greek myth and became particularly popular in the subsequent musical film *My Fair Lady*.

6 Shaw intended to use the play to campaign for the autonomy of women and was dismayed when the ending of his play was changed during production.

7 The myth has also been thought to contain the theme of 'the prostitute with a heart of gold', and depict the restitution of fallen women.

8 The myth lies behind all stories of mechanical robots or automata.

9 The myth has been used politically to support the rise of feminism.

10 The myth also plays with ideas of the relationship between art and life.

Conclusion

Down the ages the great stories within Greek mythology have been extraordinarily influential. They have reappeared time and time again in the areas of art, architecture, literature, religion and philosophy. The Romans led the way by taking over the Greek myths and adapting them to their own use, preserving them in the works of authors such as Ovid and Virgil. Since then there have been two major revivals of interest in Greek culture, the European Renaissance of the sixteenth and seventeenth centuries, and the Romantic movement of the early nineteenth century. Each time, the myths have been used to foster a new direction in thinking. The fact that they are again enjoying a new lease of life in the twenty-first century is testament to the extraordinary richness of philosophical and psychological insight that can be found in them.

Like the civilization from which they came, the Greek myths are extremely complex and sophisticated, and in their attempt to understand and explain the place of man in the universe, they are unparalleled. As a basis for religious and philosophical thinking, their influence is evident, as is demonstrated by the fact that Plato himself recounted the myth of Er when discussing the immortality of the soul. They also have connections with other systems of belief. The story of Zeus appearing to the virgin Danaë as a shower of gold links directly with the story of the Virgin Mary being visited by the Holy Spirit, while the death and resurrection of Jesus is prefigured in the Dionysian Mysteries. Again, when Demeter roams the earth searching for Persephone, there is a close correspondence with the Egyptian goddess Isis searching for her lost love, Osiris, while the dark sorceress Hecate is another form of the Russian Baba Yaga with her shrine of skulls.

Where the heroes are concerned, powerful psychological themes become apparent. These include the search for the father-figure, the acquisition of prowess, the development of inner strength and integrity, and the experience of the Underworld. Added to this, a theme which is particularly strong in Greek myth is that of the father fearing death from his son or grandson and eventually dying at the younger man's hands.

The fact that some of the heroes' adventures are bound up with historical exploration is also undisputed. Voyages such as those of Jason and Odysseus can be charted, as was proved by Tim Severin who undertook the outward journey of the Argonauts in a reconstructed *Argo*. Archaeology has revealed much that relates to the historical veracity of some of the myths, such as the discovery of the palace of Knossos on Crete and the unearthing of the ancient city of Troy.

The myths have also made their mark in the field of psychoanalysis. Freud's theory of the Oedipus complex gave rise to a fresh evaluation of the old tales in search of treasures of psychological insight; Jung raised the understanding of mythological material to new heights in terms of archetypal material, while Joseph Campbell showed how the stories of different cultures overlap one another and together offer a map of the human condition. However, Greek myths are particularly well integrated into the Western psyche, and therefore have a special power to make its workings accessible.

That this is the current gift of the Greek myths is evident, and it is to be hoped that, in terms of the exploration of relationships, the use of symbolism and the application of psychoanalytical analysis, they can continue to be regarded as a source of wisdom and instruction.

Select bibliography

Apollodorus, *The Library of Greek Mythology*, trans. Robin Hard (Oxford University Press, 1997)

Baring, Anne, and Cashford, Jules, *The Myth of the Goddess* (Penguin, 1993)

Boa, Frazer, *The Way of Myth: Talking with Joseph Campbell* (Shambhala, 1994)

Caldecott, Moyra, *Mythical Journeys, Legendary Quests* (Blandford, 1996)

Campbell, Joseph, *The Hero with a Thousand Faces* (Fontana, 1993)

Campbell, Joseph, *The Power of Myth* (Doubleday, 1991)

Fraser, James, *The Golden Bough* (Oxford Paperbacks, 2009)

Fromm, Erich, *The Forgotten Language* (Grove Press 1951)

Grant, Michael, *Myths of the Greeks and Romans* (The New American Library, 1962)

Graves, Robert, *The Greek Myths* (Penguin, 1955)

Homer, *The Odyssey*, trans. E. V. Rieu (Penguin 1946)

Husain, Shahrukh, *The Goddess* (Duncan Baird 1997)

Jung, Carl, G., *The Archetypes and the Collective Unconscious* (Routledge, 1959)

Jung, Carl, G., *Man and his Symbols* (Penguin, 1964)

Kerényi, C., *The Gods of the Greeks* (Thames and Hudson, 1951)

Kirk, G. S., *The Nature of Greek Myths* (Penguin, 1974)

March, Jenny, *Dictionary of Classical Mythology* (Cassell, 1998)

Pausanias, *Description of Greece*, trans. and ed. P. Levi (revised edn, Penguin, 1979)

Pearson, Carol S., *Awakening the Heroes Within* (HarperCollins, 1991)

Severin, Tim, *The Jason Voyage* (Hutchinson, 1985)

Schlain, Leonard, *The Alphabet versus the Goddess* (Penguin, 1998)

Perseus Project website: <u>www.perseus.tufts.edu/hopper</u>

DVD: *Joseph Campbell and The Power of Myth*, *with Bill Myers* (original PBS documentary series, originally broadcast in 1988; re-released by Athena 2010)

Index